DRINKING FOR CHAPS

GUSTAV TEMPLE has been the Editor of *The Chap* magazine since 1999 and is the author of five books, including *Cooking for Chaps*. He is an expert on social and sartorial etiquette and has appeared on TV and radio.

OLLY SMITH is an award-winning wine expert and writes a weekly column for the *Mail on Sunday's Event* magazine. He has written three books and regularly appears as wine expert on BBC1's *Saturday Kitchen* and ITV's *This Morning*. He also pops up presenting on BBC Radio 2 and internationally with his ongoing wine and travel series on the Food Network and Travel Channel.

DRINKING

for Chaps

How to Choose One's Booze

GUSTAV TEMPLE
& OLLY SMITH

PHOTOGRAPHY BY PETER CASSIDY
ILLUSTRATIONS BY JOHN BRADLEY

KYLE BOOKS

To Susannah, light of liquid fire in my glass

GUSTAV TEMPLE

To Sophie, the greatest human bottle in the global drinks cabinet

OLLY SMITH

First published in Great Britain in 2015 by
Kyle Books, an imprint of Kyle Cathie Ltd
192–198 Vauxhall Bridge Road
London SW1V 1DX
general.enquiries@kylebooks.com
www.kylebooks.com

10 9 8 7 6 5 4 3 2 1

ISBN 978 0 85783 299 3

Photographer: Peter Cassidy
Illustrator: John Bradley
Stylist: Leida Nassir-Pour
Project Editor: Sophie Allen
Copy Editor: Stephanie Evans
Editorial Assistant: Hannah Coughlin
Production: Nic Jones, Gemma John and Lisa Pinnell

A Cataloguing in Publication record for this title is available from the British Library.

Colour reproduction by ALTA London.

Printed and bound in China by C&C Offset Printing Co., Ltd.

CONTENTS

————//————

INTRODUCTION

WHEN ASKED what a gentleman should place in his drinks cabinet I have always replied, 'Booze.' This, however, would have made rather a short book, so I set myself the task of finding the perfect chap with whom to conduct a more detailed analysis. Peter O'Toole was completely dead, Shane McGowan completely drunk and Richard E. Grant completely teetotal. Who could I ask who was alive, sober – at least some of the time – and, crucially, knew in which type of glass one should serve a Pousse Café? Then I remembered a shadowy figure, occasionally spotted lurking outside my local pub. Usually clad in fur coat and winkle-pickers, he would always be seen sniffing the air outside the windows, then reaching a gloved hand from his pocket to scratch the bricks surrounding the doorway. Only very infrequently would he actually enter the pub, and then swiftly order, and consume in rapid succession, six pints of Best Bitter. Then he would leave.

It was on one of the rare occasions when he entered and I happened to be drinking in there, that I discovered what this insane fellow was up to. He had been testing the temperature of the pub's exterior, to ensure that the beer in the cellar was being kept at precisely the correct temperature. His instincts were legend. Solely by sniffing one speck of the brickwork from the Lewes Arms could this man be sure that his pint would be served in the right conditions.

That man was Olly Smith's brother-in-law's cousin, twice removed. But he introduced me to Olly once, and a nicer, more jovial fellow you could not hope to meet. And I still hope to meet him. Olly's working practice is unusual, to say the least. He drinks, he writes, then he drinks again, and occasionally dashes to the window ledge to inspect a glass of Armagnac he left there three days earlier, to test some theory or other. I once visited him at his workroom to discuss one of the chapters of this book. It was a curious building at the bottom of his garden, constructed entirely out of leather. The insulation was provided by thousands of corks ranged wine-side out along the walls, providing a musky, pungent, boozy odour. Olly greeted me at the brown leather door, clad in a pair of purple velvet pyjamas with hussar facings. 'I can only write in these,' he explained, when I cast a disapproving glance at them.

I was soon to discover, however, that there was method in Smith's madness. His legendary nose was constantly active; during our brief meeting, he would dash over to the walls and slightly adjust one of the corks, claiming that the aroma from the cork of a 25-year-old bottle of port was bothering him. I had brought a bottle of champagne as a gift. Olly inspected the exterior, read the label, opened it with a vast Cavalry officer's sword, then poured the entire contents out of the window. 'Thank you,' he merely said, offering me a cup of herbal tea.

This Quixotic fellow has proved difficult, unpunctual, exasperating and downright rude to work with – but the knowledge that pours forth from him, not to mention the wine that pours forth from his cellar when he's feeling generous, has made it all worth it. Olly has led me to the realisation that there is nothing shameful about knowing a bit more about alcohol than simply how much one can tolerate. Far from blinding me with the frilly pomposity of the wine snob, he has shown me, and together we shall hopefully show you, that drinking and enjoying alcoholic beverages is one of the true essential arts of the gentleman. Along with fencing, riding to hounds, smoking a pipe, dressing exceedingly well, doffing one's hat and being excessively courteous to the ladies, the art of drinking should be mastered to the highest possible level. I sincerely hope that this book will assist you in that endeavour.

GUSTAV TEMPLE

'LOATHSOME' is not a word I would use to describe my final meeting with Gustav before submitting the manuscript for this book. 'Belligerent' is more accurate. If Krakatoa and Mount Etna pitched together to decide who could belch the hottest, the encounter would make my editorial meetings with Gustav look like Lord's, home of cricket, silently becalmed in a subtle dusting of December snow. If you've watched the opening episode of *The Persuaders*, in which Roger Moore and Tony Curtis destroy Monte Carlo's Hôtel de Paris in a fist fight over whether the Creole Scream cocktail is to be served with one olive or two, you'll know exactly what I'm talking about.

'Which spirit sold more than twice as much as any other in 2013?' Gustav verbally fast-bowled at me from his copper bathtub. (He insists on bathing now whenever we meet, to keep instantly clean from any of my 'infernal contaminations', and he always wears a diving helmet in my presence.) 'Jinro Soju from Korea,' I defended with my cover drive of a succinctly accurate reply. Distilled from rice, I only tasted this curious beverage in the first place because Gustav dared me to find a flavour that he'd never before slurped, at the peak of one of our many excruciating battles during the writing of this book. The Soju I sampled was delicious, in spite of Gustav's spurious claim that he 'invented the stuff' on a childhood trip to Korea. The hidden popularity of this drink, thanks, in part, to the support of Korean superstar Psy, is extraordinary and we firmly intend to do the same for many of the drinks in these pages, from Warner Edwards Harrington Gin to Regal Rogue Vermouth. In truth, we have come to adore such drinks as a pair of mother dragons smouldering over their nest of fiery eggs. And this is especially true of Campari. But how did the eruptive and unlikely union that sent this book hurtling hotly into the literary skies all begin?

The process of writing this book has been as mysterious as it has been illuminating. I have discovered, for example, that Gustav is prone to disguising himself as himself – very confusing during meetings in his underground bunker crammed full of effigies and busts of his own face. He will tell you that I insist on arriving at Chap HQ riding a stuffed Friesian cow on wheels with a hose

spraying a gentle mist of salt water from the heavens. This is only partially true. The mist is, in fact, Fino sherry. And the Friesian is very much alive, though, I admit, is terribly slow. If I had to praise Gustav on a single detail of his fastidiously enterprising and enduring talents, it would undoubtedly be his ability to taste, judge and then execute his opinion with all the precision, charm and the ruthlessness of an adder throttling a bluebottle. I dare say he would single out my punctuality as the only praiseworthy asset in my personal armoury.

Never in any collaboration have I been subjected to quite as much dressing up, sampling of snuff and quoting of long-dead noble Romans. Yet, in truth, it has been a blast. The drinks in these pages have enlarged our spheres of joy and appreciation and we have come to love the sheer hugeness of it all. The flavours locked in these pages are as diverse and elusive as the very webs of ether that hold our planet in the sky like an ice cube rattling around in a tumbler of dark matter. Mankind's inventiveness with flavour, with strength and with the curious intent to expand the mind with tinctures of naughtiness have, at times, rendered us both elated and sleepy in equal measure, a state which we have come to describe as 'Dozing Divine'.

Of course we have probably been arrested over a hundred times for brawling and duelling during the creation of this lexicon of crumpled lies and polished cheer but, I think you'll agree, 'tis a small price to pay for the tome of wonderment that we are delighted to present to you here today. Enough words have been spilled on the subject of our lusty enterprise. This book is quite simply for you. We thank you for picking it up. We commend its pages to your eyeballs and hope with the sincerest of sincerity, whether it is a spirit, wine, beer, cocktail or fortified dream of destructive splendour that results from our words to your glass that your smile is wider, your heart beats brighter and your vim is pruned into a topiary of more defined delight.

Our glasses are raised to yours, which we earnestly entreat always to be full.

OLLY SMITH

'Gentlemen, I have just met with the most extraordinary adventure that ever occurred to a human being. As I was walking along the Grassmarket, all of a sudden the street rose up and struck me on the face.'

THE HON. ALEXANDER GORDON, LORD ROCKVILLE

DRINKS CABINET
OF CURIOSITIES

Perhaps the most important and impertinent question, before we begin to fill it, is what a chap's drinks cabinet should look like. The essential components of a gentleman's drinks cabinet are as follows.

First of all, the cabinet itself. Size is of the essence, for, unless you are a dipsomaniac, your drinks collection generally increases in quantity, at least in terms of bottles rather than how much is in them. Always allow your booze furniture to expand its collection by at least six bottles per month – this could arrive in the form of gifts, duty-free shops and holidays, or simply on the delicious whims one experiences when idly grazing the aisles of one's local vintner.

By all means go vintage and purchase a stylish 1950s cocktail cabinet, complete with flashing lights and secret compartments, but assume that just the one will never be enough to house a decent cellar. Those novelty items were generally made back in the days when people drank a lot more out of the house than in. Elegance and functionality are your watchwords, and bear in mind that this item of furniture is a whole lot more than a cupboard. This is your wardrobe to Narnia and as such it should never be:

> In any way 'retro', 'upcycled' or 'shabby chic'. These are words used by imbeciles to describe things they have spent money on which should probably have been free.

> Too small. You are a drinker and you should be as proud of it as Prometheus was of his flaming prong.

> Discreet. See above. Flame. Prong.

> Too low. When reaching for your best bottle of Pineau des Charentes, you want to stand on both of your hind legs engaging in scintillating conversation, revealing your candour and class with the merest hint of malevolent intrigue. Never crawl or crouch to fetch a bottle. You should employ people to do that sort of thing for you.

> Locked. That would be utterly weird.

Your serried ranks of bottles should include but not be limited to the following:

FOR COCKTAILS & MIXED DRINKS

Vermouth
Blended whisky
Rye whiskey (American or Canadian)
Bourbon whiskey
Gin
Vodka
Dark rum
Light rum
Spanish brandy
Pisco
Grappa
Kahlua
Campari
Aperol
Triple Sec/Cointreau/Grand Marnier
Absinthe
Bitters
Orange bitters

FOR STRAIGHT SIPPAGE

Armagnac
Cognac
Single malt whisky
Additional bourbon
An assortment of worldwide whiskies
Fine tequila and mezcal
Madeira
Tawny port

SOFT DRINKS

Tonic water (Fever Tree)
Soda water
Ginger ale (Fever Tree)
Ginger beer
Lemonade
Grenadine and a selection of cordials
Every fruit juice known to man

FRUITS

Fresh lemons
Fresh limes
Jar of Maraschino cherries
Jar of olives
Jar of silverskin onions

ICE

Tons of it

EQUIPMENT

HARDWARE

One stainless steel or glass cocktail
    shaker
Strainer
Jigger (two-sized metal measuring
    vessel)
At least six ice trays
Barspoons or cocktail stirrer, made of
    metal or glass
Muddler (tool for mashing ingredients
    in a glass)
Large glass jug in which to mix drinks

GLASSWARE

Tumblers – for whisky

Highball glasses – for mixed drinks
such as G&T

Tulip glasses – for neat sippage of
vodka, single malt, rum etc.

Wine glasses – with lip curving in at the
top. (Olly has designed The Glass
which is impeccable for both red and
white and available via the Interweb.)

Champagne flutes – though many these
days prefer fine champagne from
white wine glasses to maximize
indulgence in the complexity of
aromas and flavours.

Shot glasses

Sherry glasses

Cocktail glasses

THE DICTIONARY OF USEFUL UTTERANCES TO DESCRIBE YOUR GUEST'S INEBRIATION
Without Them Necessarily Realising that the Drinks Cabinet is Closing

HE/SHE IS

Sipping from the chalice of regret.
On the slow train to Barbados.
Brewing his/her own kidney beer.
As romantic as an angry bear.
Very capable.
Has a verruca on his/her brain.
Riding the cat.
A wig on the wrong head.
Devil friendly.
Squinting like a goat.
Hoisting the trouserleg flag.
Snake dancing.
Cold kettle.
Has taken front row debentures at his/
her own match.
Sucking a coconut.
Pharaoh's deathbed whim.
Sunbathing in Moscow.
Doing quite well.
At variance with the league of
humanity.
Well spoken.

Keep these written on a card inside the
Drinks Cabinet of Curiosities in case you
need to discreetly point at one of them
ruefully when Aunt Ada has snaffled one too
many of your Gin Biscuits.

Never make Gin Biscuits.

CHAPTER 1

COCKTAILS & CLOWNERY

THE ORIGIN of the word 'cocktail' remains a completely baffling mystery to historians. One minute men were swigging fermented fruit from gourds and grunting at each other, the next they were swapping witticisms while sipping Gibsons from delicate glasses adorned with daintily speared tiny onions. Undoubtedly pirates had something to do with this vast stride into sophistication, for there is more than a whiff of the high seas and palm-fringed islands about a cocktail, and pirates would inevitably end up with random selections of looted barrels of booze, which they may or may not have chucked into glasses with frosted sugar around the rims.

Cocktails as we know them entered history at just about the same time as true chaps did, i.e. in the 1920s. Before that, chaps were in their early stages, still wearing frilly neckerchiefs and rather over-informative britches. Their choice of drink, before the invention of the Dry Martini, would have been brandy, port or both – but equal measures of port and brandy, while being an excellent palliative for the common cold, can hardly be classed as a cocktail. Unless you are Oliver Reed during the small hours of the morning after a night of carousing and cajoling, in which case it can be classed as 'The Sun Riser'.

The Jazz Age, F. Scott Fitzgerald and Prohibition were the three principal factors that ushered cocktails into public life. The hectic rhythm of Dixieland Jazz required its followers to jump around a lot – much easier with a few Sidecars under your belt than a flagon of ale; F. Scott's elegant chronicles of the age relied extensively on highballs and martinis to maintain the pace (as did the man himself for most of his short life); and Prohibition, having banned all the proper booze, unwittingly brought about the production of illegal 'hooch' – undrinkable spirits, which could only be guzzled in decent quantities by disguising them with sugar, fruit juices and the like.

Once America decided to allow its citizens to drink alcohol again, cocktails hung around, though vastly improved and less dangerous to drink, as they now contained decent shots of officially sanctioned spirits. They went through an aesthetically questionable phase in the 1950s, when gentlemen sported Hawaiian shirts and played the bongos. This was a dark decade in other ways too, when the Piña Colada and the Tequila Sunrise were born – but things picked up again in the 1980s, when expensive cocktails suited the profligacy and showing off that was rampant in financial districts across the globe, just as it had been in the 1920s before the Wall Street Crash.

Cocktails have recently gone through what the drinks industry calls 'a renaissance', which simply means they have become more

A skating waiter at The Grand Hotel, St Moritz

expensive. Walk into a trendy cocktail bar in London's East End these days and you are likely to be offered a glass full of blue liquid billowing with steam, and handed some asbestos gloves with which to drink it. As all good chaps know, the invention of cocktails, like the invention of wine, was a defining moment for mankind and does not need to be revisited. Once the list of staples had been achieved, a full century ago, the only way that cocktail-making needs to be developed is by occasional experimentation. By that we mean using rum instead of whisky in a Manhattan, or mezcal instead of gin in your Negroni – as opposed to plunging your cocktail shaker into a vat of nitrogen and jabbering more excitedly than Doctor Emmett Brown from *Back to the Future*.

What chap has not tired of entering a cocktail bar and, perusing the 'menu' (there shouldn't even be one, unless you are going to have a Brandy Alexander for dinner), finding only unfamiliar concoctions with absurd names that bear no relation to anything in his life, such as 'Dude Where's My Sidecar', 'Pass the Dutchie' and 'Chillax Mate It Might Never Happen'. One should simply enter a cocktail bar with a small selection of classic cocktails imprinted on one's mind, choose the right one for the occasion and for your lady companion – as a rule, chaps don't drink cocktails with each other; that's the job of beer when not entertaining at home – and command the bartender to make it. If he knows his silverskin onions, he will silently and professionally approach his task, and in all likelihood be glad of the opportunity to display the skills he learned, many years previously, at the Great University of Bartending.

So, what are the essential cocktails that should fill one's own personal cocktail menu of the mind? It is important to distinguish this from the ones you know how to make yourself, which is a completely different list. Certainly, feel free to shake your dinner guests a Martini at home, or hand round the Daiquiris at a garden party, but they should be distinct from the ones you know how to order in a bar with authority.

On a chill winter's eve, huddled in a cosy bar in a cold northern European city, a Manhattan will go down nicely. In fact, a Manhattan will always go down nicely. Some cocktail novices can be disappointed when, having ordered something with a fancy name like 'A Thousand and One Nights of Passion', the bright orange concoction is delivered in an ordinary half pint glass with a straw sticking out of it, and not even a Maraschino cherry. A Manhattan is whiskey based, always served in a cocktail glass, is a lovely dark woody colour and tastes of Dixieland Jazz. A Mint Julep, on the other hand, is one for a summer afternoon. Based around bourbon, it is the deep Southern State sister to the Cuban Mojito (rum based, read on) and the official tipple of the Kentucky Derby. Of course, it featured as a supporting role

in the James Bond film *Goldfinger*. Auric Goldfinger offers Bond a Mint Julep at his Kentucky stud farm, to which Bond replies 'sour mash, not too sweet'. An Old Fashioned is more of a meal than a drink, and involves a slice of orange, Maraschino cherries, bitters and sugar, all drowned in bourbon and served in a tumbler. Those are the only three bourbon-based cocktails you need to know, unless you want a tall glass of whiskey and soda with a cherry in it – in which case order a John Collins.

ESSENTIAL COCKTAILS

————— // —————

MANHATTAN: 50ml whiskey, 25ml sweet vermouth, a dash of angostura bitters mixed with ice. Strain into a cocktail glass and garnish with a twist of orange or a Maraschino cherry.

MINT JULEP: Served traditionally in a silver or pewter cup to keep it cool, but these days it rarely is. A tall glass will do. Add a handful of fresh mint leaves, a jot of sugar syrup and gently muddle with the leaves until you can smell the mint. Don't crush too hard or the mint will become over-powering. Fill the glass with ice cubes and add as much or as little bourbon as you feel like. A sprig of fresh mint is an optional garnish.

GIN COCKTAILS

These are probably the most important set, principally because your lady companion will usually require something lighter than bourbon, Scotch or brandy, not as vulgar as vodka (Vodka Red Bull has almost destroyed the reputation of vodka, though we will do our best to save it) and not as ridiculous as a Tequila Sunrise. The most classic of all cocktails is of course the Dry Martini, and this is one you really have to know how to order properly, otherwise the bartender will start showing off. (Gustav recalls asking for a Dry Martini in a country hotel and the Italian barman got very excited and delivered a hostess trolley to the table with several types of gin, bowls of olives, lemons and a perfume sprayer. There was no bottle of vermouth because that was in the perfume sprayer. After much fussing and flourishing, Gustav was presented with a Martini-flavoured eau de toilette.)

SIR KINGSLEY SAYS *'With all respect to James Bond, a Martini should be stirred, not shaken. Shakers are far too small ... a shaker about the size of a hatbox might be worth pondering, but I have never seen or heard of such.'*

Similarly President Jed Bartlet of *The West Wing* fame says 'Shaken, not stirred, will get you cold water with a dash of gin and dry vermouth. The reason you stir it with a special spoon is so not to chip the ice. James Bond is ordering a weak martini and being snooty about it.'

Bartenders appreciate customers who know what they want much more than people who want to be impressed. If you

American cocktail bar, 1930s

order a Dry Martini, specify a precise ratio of gin to vermouth and specify both the brand of gin and vermouth – Tanqueray (widely available) and Noilly Prat is a timeless combination, though if you want to appear completely uninterested in fashion, request Plymouth gin, Britain's oldest gin distillery.

'Barkeeper, a Warner Edwards Dry Martini please, as dry as the Sahara with a lemon twist. Stirred not shaken. Have a second one standing by, I'm travelling Thirst Class'. Whoever said that got it right. Stirring rather than shaking will preserve more flavour, since shaking dilutes with ice.

DRY MARTINI: Cocktail books from the Jazz Age specify a modest-sounding ratio of five parts gin to two parts vermouth, while modern ratios can treat vermouth like some sort of homoeopathic medicine. Ian Fleming's version falls somewhere in the middle and is therefore probably perfect: three measures of Gordon's, one of vodka, half a measure of Kina Lillet. Feel free to order a Dirty Martini with a splash of salty olive brine, but be aware that this will mark you out as a cad. Even Bond baulked at Martinis that were unclean in any way. And besides, you're paying for gin, not brackish water. For the optimum ratio of gin to Martini, we recommend 65ml gin to 10ml Martini. If you're making a large batch, roughly six parts gin to one part Martini.

THE GIBSON: Similar to a Dry Martini, but instead of an olive or a twist of lemon, usually it contains three cocktail onions. Ordering one of these will mark you out as a man who plays by his own rules, especially if you insist on New York's Four Seasons' ratio of three parts gin to half a measure of vermouth. Cocktails for two can be given a nice balance by ordering a Dry Martini or Gibson for yourself and a Negroni for her: gin, Campari, red vermouth with a twist of orange peel. It is essential to use the best gin and the top red vermouth – which we believe to be Antica Formula. Naturally you can swap these around between the sexes at will, but it might be a good place to start the evening.

SINGAPORE SLING: Still with gin, the Singapore Sling remains a stylish summer cocktail and one particularly favoured by the ladies, as it isn't too strong and the only manly thing about it is that it is always served in a highball glass. Definitely a first date drink to order for a lady unsure about her cocktails. Invented by Ngiam Tong Boon, head bartender of the Raffles Hotel Singapore, in the 1900s. The original recipe was very nearly lost to folklore. These days there are many adaptations featuring pineapple juice, Grenadine, Cointreau and more, but we prefer ours a tad less fruity: 25ml gin, 25ml cherry brandy, 25ml Benedictine, 25ml lime juice, an optional dash of angostura and squirt of soda water. Serve in a tall glass with a twist of lime.

GIN FIZZ: Fulfilling a very similar function to the Singapore sling is the Gin Fizz. 50ml gin, the juice of ½ lemon, sugar to taste (we take 1 teaspoon) serve in a tumbler with ice cubes and top up with soda water.

BRANDY COCKTAILS

These straddle the sexual divide and can be a nice way of sharing an experience with a lady, as they contain something for everybody. A Sidecar, hailing from the Prohibition era, comes in a cocktail glass and contains nothing but cognac, Cointreau and fresh sour mix (something bartenders make in advance and which you don't need to know how to make, unless you want to become a bartender). Brandy Alexanders were the drink of choice for Evelyn Waugh's character Anthony Blanche in *Brideshead Revisited*. They perfectly reflect Blanche's saucy, continental, shifty loucheness, as he guzzles one after another and reveals the truth about Sebastian Flyte to the book's narrator. A much heavier, wintry cocktail than any of the above, it contains cognac, crème de cacao and cream and is sprinkled with nutmeg. Two Brandy Alexanders and you can skip dinner altogether. Finally, a Classic Stinger, popular in literary salons of the 1930s, comes in a tumbler and contains brandy and white crème de menthe and is always served with a glass of iced water as a chaser (or should be).

RUM COCKTAILS

These immediately transport one to the Caribbean and are ideally consumed on those very islands. The next best thing is to drink them in a cavernous cocktail bar with lots of dark wood panelling and potted palms – if you can find one outside Havana. Mojitos work well in the summer, though they have become somewhat ubiquitous: mint sprigs floating in a deep mixture of white rum, crushed ice, sugar and lime juice. For a more exotic kick, a Mai Tai blends dark rum with triple sec, amaretto, grenadine and lime juice. See, you're already half way across the Atlantic just hearing those words, aren't you? Finally, a Daiquiri, usually served in a white wine glass, but can be requested in a cocktail glass to maintain decorum, originally contained nothing more than rum, fresh lime juice and sugar but these days seems to encompass the entire realm of fruit-fuelled liqueurs.

When making cocktails at home, you're much better off avoiding any of these classics – leave them to the professionals. Have more fun creating your own concoctions, following a few basic principles: never use more than three spirits in one cocktail, stick to drinks that are roughly the same colour and use tons of ice in the shaker: a warm Martini does not feature in any of the James Bond books. We have created a modest selection of our top ten chap cocktails for you to try at home:

THE ANARCHO-DANDY GUZZLER

50ml Spanish brandy or cognac
15ml fresh lemon juice
15ml grenadine
50ml pineapple juice (optional)
A drop of orange blossom water

Shake and strain over crushed ice in a tumbler and infuse with memories of comfortably salacious undergarments.

BUTTON UP YOUR OVERCOAT

50ml blended Scotch (e.g. Johnnie Walker Black Label)
15ml sweet red vermouth
10ml dry vermouth

Stir over ice while whistling the National Anthem and serve in a Martini glass. Garnish with lemon peel.

DING DONG!

50ml gold rum
15ml fresh lime
2 dashes Angostura bitters
5ml absinthe
ginger beer, to top up

Mix ingredients in a highball glass and top up with ginger beer. If you're feeling brave, garnish with a stick of fresh ginger.

PHARAOH'S BLUFF

50ml Plymouth gin
5ml dry vermouth
10ml Green Chartreuse

Prepare as a normal Gin Martini and serve in a glass rinsed with the Green Chartreuse. Garnish with blue cheese-stuffed olives. But remember – even numbers of olives are bad luck and will invoke the Pharoah's curse.

STEADY ON, JEEVES

25ml Plymouth gin
25ml Campari
25ml sweet red vermouth
50ml prosecco

Mix in a tumbler, serve over ice and garnish with a slice of orange, carefully carved into the shape of an English moustache.

THE GREASY POLE

50ml vodka
75ml beef consommé (chilled)
dash of Worcestershire sauce
dash of Tabasco sauce
squeeze of lemon

Mix in a highball glass over ice. If you're feeling daring, add a dollop of horseradish sauce.

SUSANNAH SLAMMER

50ml Spanish brandy
50ml Cointreau
Splash of peach schnapps
Juice of 1 lime

Shake over ice, strain into a tall glass with 1 ice cube and top with ginger ale.

IT'S NOT A RUFF, IT'S MY NECK

50ml rye whiskey
ginger ale
a whole lemon

Mix the rye and ginger ale in a highball glass over ice, then carefully trim the peel from your whole lemon and spiral it into the glass. Applaud yourself with every sip.

CHURCHILL'S RESURRECTION

bottle of dry vermouth
50ml London dry gin

Salute the bottle of vermouth with your bottle of gin, but make sure not to get it too close. Pour the gin over ice and stir 21 times anticlockwise. Strain into a frozen Martini glass and garnish with a lemon twist.

THE ALMANAC OF ACTION

25ml Plymouth gin
25ml Cointreau
25ml Lillet/dry vermouth
15ml fresh lemon juice
5ml absinthe

Shake and strain into a chilled coupe or Martini glass. Garnish with a lemon twist. Laugh out loud at just how splendid life is.

With thanks to **Off Broadway**,
63–65 Broadway Market, London, E8 4PH
www.offbroadway.org.uk

DRESSING FOR DRINK

◆

Cocktails should always be consumed in evening dress, preferably with a cream, rather than black, dinner jacket. If cream is unavailable, then midnight blue will do – which is designed to look jet black under artificial light. When drinking cocktails, you will always be under artificial light, whether beneath the chandeliers of the Grand Casino at Monte Carlo or lurking near the neon strip lights in a Berlin speakeasy. The loosened bow tie gives an admittedly louche air, and for this reason is only permitted after midnight. You may wear a fez, but only with a cream dinner jacket and only if located south of Cadiz or east of Constantinople.

CHAPTER 2

THE BUBBLY BALLOON
Champagne & Sparkling Wine

EVERY CHAP should relish the mystery of fizz, while simultaneously glorifying its entirely explicable origins. Much of the champagne talk is in devilish code, from 'échelle' to 'cru', but with an informal explanation of what it all means, you'll be able to tell the good from the best, the overpriced and the undervalued. English fizz, we reveal, belongs in every chap's bloodstream. Almost certainly most of the time. Buying champagne, serving champagne and deciphering their infernal labels will all become as clear to you as the crystal waters of the River Know-How. And let's also turn our taste buds towards cava and prosecco – strictly for drinking at home, in private and acceptably with guests on first-name terms. Buck's Fizz is, naturally, only acceptable during the morning. Any chap found with a Buck's Fizz at his fingertips post-midday commits the crime of 'juicing the pips', resulting in a most bitter and punishing curse.

Sparkling wine was, of course, invented by an Englishman in England and is, in some ways, the most English of drinks, mimicking our eccentricity with effortless effervescence. In 1662, Christopher Merret presented a paper to the Royal Society on how to make wine 'brisk and sparkling'. That's at least 30 years before a monk called Dom Pérignon is said to have invented sparkling wine in Hautvilliers in a country called 'France'. Chaps internationally are unanimous that the name Christopher Merret should be heralded with as much glory, trump and splendour as sharing a cigar with Winston Churchill, a sensibly strong dose of winter knitwear and gargling the good times away on the pristine coastline of Mexico's Riviera Maya.

First of all, to discern a top-notch glass of bubbly from merely a flaccid white wine that's been injected with helium, one searches, yearns and insists upon the following:

HISTORY & CONJECTURE *Pol Roger, Winston Churchill's preferred champagne house, made a special one-pint bottle of champagne, to be served to our famous bon viveur every day at 11am. Conjecture varies as to the exact number of bottles he consumed but we are certain that the number is heroic. It's been reported that he consumed 42,000 bottles of Champagne in his lifetime. What a chap.*

Marilyn Monroe, 1953

The tiniest bubbles imaginable; ones that would make a pinhead feel like an ogre.

More bubbles than are strictly necessary.

A delicately creamy and cascading sensation when sipped. If a single bubble dares to prickle in the manner of Club Soda, the beverage must immediately be rejected, if not hurled at your host, in favour of a comforting and restorative pint of golden ale. Alone.

CONJECTURE *Marilyn Monroe allegedly took a bath in 350 bottles' worth of champagne. Where's a high-dive when you need one?*

Opening the thing is child's play and any garish oaf caught popping corks to make the sound of an octopus giving birth to a bullet is a burglar of behaviour. Popping the cork risks spillage and wastage but furthermore shocks the bubbles into submission. It's taken effort, care and craft cunningly to weave them into this elixir of jovial sparkle, and the most respectful method of opening is also the safest:

STEP 1: Remove the foil, cage and capsule from around the cork.

STEP 2: Grasp the cork, turning the bottle gently on to its side.

STEP 3: If the bottle is wet with condensation, use a tea towel to grip the bottle.

STEP 4: Turn the bottle, not the cork, and apply pressure to control the cork.

STEP 5: Release the cork as gently as possible. The maximum noise acceptable is the sigh of an overworked bank teller.

When serving fizz, coupe glasses are to be avoided at all costs. They may look the part but they maximise the surface area and result in the regrettably efficient dispersal of bubbles. Flutes are traditionally the preferred way to ensure a tantalisingly focused burst of aroma, but a chap should also consider deploying the glory of a white wine glass for particularly special bottles of champagne, providing you remember only to fill the wine up to the point of return, where the bowl of the glass first turns back inward – the widest point in the glass – and no higher. This enables spill-free swirling and an even dispersal of aromas to enhance and maximise your nasal pleasure.

But before we even get to serving sparkling wines and champagne at the correct temperature (between 8 and 10°C) there is a quagmire of gibberish to be un-muddled and easily de-riddled across sparkling wine labels, to ensure that every chap selects the brightest bubbly for the optimum occasion. First of all, there are different methods for making different types of fizz:

PROSECCO, which is as Italian as it sounds, is made by the less-expensive 'Tank' or 'Charmat method', which takes the name of the French inventor Eugène Charmat. Still white wine undergoes a secondary fermentation under pressure in a tank before bottling. The wine is usually softer and more fruity and the bubbles are larger than in fizz made under the 'Traditional Method' or 'Champagne Method'. With the Traditional Method, the all-important secondary fermentation takes place inside every individual bottle, resulting in a more elegantly textured fizz of greater finesse. Cava, English sparkling wine and of course champagne are all made under the labour-intensive and far more costly Traditional Method.

Alas, the differences do not end there. Prosecco is made from the soft fruity Glera grape in northern Italy near the town of Treviso. For the top-notch kit, look for DOCG on the label and for the stellar stuff (which, it's worth noting, is even more fruity and less dry than other proseccos) hunt the word 'Cartizze' on the label, which denotes a very small production area that provides some of the very best conditions for this grape. Prosecco can of course be deployed in cocktails with fruit purées, most notably peach to make a Bellini. But cordials too make it a champion of impromptu pop – our favourite is homemade rhubarb cordial for a late autumn dose of pink tasty tang to the drink. So far as food goes, light bites rule the roost, from salads to fritto misto, but a few torn hunks of fresh mozzarella with a glass of cool prosecco is summertime's optimum snack.

CAVA is made in Spain, usually from the local Spanish grape varieties – Macabeo, Parellada and Xarel-lo. Unlike prosecco, it is made by the Traditional Method, resulting in a sparkling wine of excellent value that can be worth cellaring – top examples develop a more mellow and savoury stratum of flavours and aromas. When young, its gently aromatic edge makes it a perfect partner to sip with a green olive, almost like wine's answer to the Dirty Martini. These days, Chardonnay and Pinot Noir are also permitted in the blend – international grapes that form the backbone of France's champagne. Cava used to be exclusively Catalonian, produced around Barcelona, but these days you can find demarcated cava areas all over Spain, though production is still small beer compared with the lands around Barcelona. Raventós I Blanc remains our cava producer of choice, but it's also worth asking your local independent wine shop for a good recommendation from a smaller producer. More widely available examples from Codorníu are also decent, though it's worth picking out their top bottlings and spending those few pennies more.

———————

MAKING CORDIALS *Cordials provide the simplest and most varied arsenal to concoct doctored deliciousness from your drinks cabinet. Take equal parts sugar and water and heat in a pan. Add the fruit or herb of your choice (or try a mixture), from rhubarb to thyme, and make sure it's covered by the liquid. Simmer gently, taste and, when the flavours make you want to sing with pleasure, strain into a bottle, allow to cool and refrigerate until required. Hint: it's easy to over-extract herbs, especially, and the pips of soft fruits such as raspberries can give a certain bitter edge, so taste as you go and strain at the optimum moment. A chap always trusts his taste buds!*

———————

Gustav only serves prosecco and cava at home in private or very occasionally to tailors with whom he is on first fitting terms. Olly serves these drinks al fresco during his Priapic Picnics of the summer months. All are welcome.

———————

THE CHAMPAGNE REGION

Of course, where fizz is concerned, the Earl Haig, the Taj Mahal, the full beans of bubbly is, of course, champagne. Synonymous with good times and glory the world over, champagne takes its name from the region in northern France where this elixir of awesomeness is concocted. Champagne is principally made from two black grapes, Pinot Noir and Pinot Meunier – which respectively give richness and fruit flavours to the blend – and the white grape Chardonnay, which is the bright star, the zip, zing and dazzle in the depth of your glass. The black grapes are pressed gently to avoid extracting colour. All colour in red wine comes from maceration of the juice with the skins. In champagne this is shunned, except in making rosé champagne, which can also be made by blending red and white wines together.

When sourcing the best champagne, the first thing you're likely to come across is brands. Here are two of the most well-known, together with an indication of their non-vintage house style.

BOLLINGER James Bond's preferred tipple in the films, a rich deep round style of champagne. Excellent with nibbles.

POL ROGER One of the most traditional champagne houses, where attention to detail is prized and creates a fresh style of elegant champagne. The perfect aperitif.

Of course, every chap will have his preferred marque of champagne, but for a couple of names that will delight your guests, feast your eyeballs on two names: **Delamotte** and **Charles Heidsieck**.

DELAMOTTE is one of the oldest champagne houses, kicking off in 1760 in the highly rated village of Le Mesnil. It is the sister house of Salon (top notch) which is only produced in exceptional vintages. Where Salon will plunder your pocket, Delamotte is more reasonably priced but still delivers wines of immense elegance and finesse. Their importers are Corney & Barrow, who sell direct through their website, which saves you on the heavy lifting.

CHARLES HEIDSIECK was the original champagne Charlie (see right). In our view the wines have in recent years undergone a huge rise in quality and across the board have been sweeping awards. In style Heidsieck champagnes are gloriously poised between opulence and elegance.

But beyond brands and names, the terminology of champagne needs to be deciphered, to ensure you know you're getting the appropriate level of enthralment and at the correct price. No point in paying for a pig's ear if you're expecting a horn-rimmed hearing trumpet.

CHAMPAGNE CHARLIES *There were two Champagne Charlies: the first was Charles-Camille Heidsieck, a dapper Frenchman who first introduced champagne to America in the mid-19th century. His promotional visits to that nation proved so successful that customers would request a 'bottle of Charles' in restaurants. Like all dandies, he had his clothes made on Savile Row, despite living in Reims, and when his tailor tried to sue him for unpaid bills, Charlie claimed that for him to be seen wearing the firm's clothes was much better for the tailor's business than having his bills settled.*

During the American Civil War, Heidsieck got himself into a pickle by crossing the Mason–Dixon line to try to get unpaid bills from Southern wine merchants settled. He wound up imprisoned by General Benjamin 'Beast' Butler on charges of espionage, and was only released when both Napoleon III and Abraham Lincoln intervened. The drama came to be known as the Heidsieck Incident. All chaps, in our opinion, should have an incident named after them.

The other Champagne Charlie was George Leybourne. This dandy singer evolved a new type of music hall artiste, the 'Lion Comique': a dashing, well-dressed man-about-town – or a 'swell'. He would appear on stage in white tie and tails, singing songs about the joys of champagne, women and the high life. In 1866, with composer Alfred Lee, he wrote 'Champagne Charlie', and within a few months it became a massive music hall hit that would be forever linked to George Leybourne's name. But George was a bit of a Champagne Charlie himself, and his relentless quest for ladies, good times and fizz resulted in his premature death in Islington aged just 42.

CHAMPAGNE TERMINOLOGY

Champagne is a riddle to be unpicked. Happily all of the information you need is plainly described on every label. Here is your handy tool to de-hieroglyph.

NV OR NON-VINTAGE. These wines have been blended across several years. This enables champagne houses to maintain a consistent style year in year out.

VINTAGE. Indicates a champagne made with grapes all cropped in one specific year that will reflect the conditions of that vintage. A vintage champagne ought to indicate that it is from an outstanding year, but the qualities will vary. For example, 2003 was a very hot year, producing unusually plump sweet grapes. Not a fantastic year if you'd like your champagne to be sharp as a lemon in a pin-stripe suit; 2004 is a better bet for chaps.

PREMIER CRU OR 1ER CRU. These are wines that are sourced from the 41 first class villages whose growing conditions are considered to produce wines of great finesse.

GRAND CRU. These are the holy villages in champagne, the vineyards that are considered to be the top of the tree. There are only 17 of these stellar sites and their wines are considered to be the best of the best.

PRESTIGE CUVÉE. A Prestige Cuvée is considered the epitome of a champagne house. For example, Moët & Chandon produces the famous Dom Pérignon. Among the very best, in our opinion, is Taittinger Comtes de Champagnes, a treat to be savoured with as much relish as one's first trip to Lord's.

EVEN MORE HISTORY & CONJECTURE
According to several manuscripts, Fredrick the Great of Prussia apparently used to drink an unusual mixture of champagne and coffee to calm his nerves. Pervert.

A note on consumption. It's quite clear that one should only drink proper champagne when celebrating something – this could be anything from the birth of your first, second or third child (if you've gone for a fourth you won't be able to afford anything stronger than Tizer, I'm afraid) to watching the first Briton to land on Venus on a television screen implanted on your fingernail in the future. However, don't treat it with too much reverence; in fact perfect the art of releasing the cork so well that, when you do open a bottle to celebrate some occasion, your companions will observe you doing so with the air of one who opens a bottle of champagne every day. Champagne is one of the few drinks that can travel anywhere; no hotel room bathroom is complete until you have filled the sink with ice and inserted at least one bottle of fizz. Champagne can be drunk while riding a camel, swimming (the only time it is acceptable to drink it from the bottle), on reaching the summit of Kilimanjaro, in a hot-air balloon and in a kayak approaching the lip of a waterfall (but only if you are the passenger – the captain will require something stronger).

'Champagne is one of the elegant extras in life.' CHARLES DICKENS

ENGLISH SPARKLING WINE

————//————

English sparkling wine deserves high praise, not for patriotism but for passionate splendour. Aside from sparkling wine being invented by an Englishman (sound the trump, toss your hat into the air and kiss an American serviceman) the quality of English – and Welsh – sparkling wine has been rising remarkably in recent years. The turning point came with the Queen's Jubilee, the Royal Wedding, the Olympics and the birth of not one but two mini-Royals. All of these events threaded across the drinking diary allowed chaps everywhere to feel a sense of confidence and pride in drinking the effervescence of our islands. Rightly so, as our climate differs little from the Champagne region, our know-how is state-of-the-art and our vineyards have intriguing – and varied – characteristics to create a wealth of styles. In the main, the headline grapes used in the Champagne region are used for top kit in England – Chardonnay (freshness), Pinot Noir (richness) and Pinot Meunier (fruitiness). Top producers that belong in every chap's arsenal include:

Gusbourne Estate (Kent)
Ridgeview (East Sussex)
Nyetimber (West Sussex)
Wiston (West Sussex)
Coates & Seely (Hampshire)
Hattingley Valley (Hampshire)
Furleigh Estate (Dorset)
Camel Valley (Cornwall)

The unique hallmark of our awesome bubbly is its arresting freshness. With temperatures on average around one degree cooler than the Champagne region, our home-grown grapes are bursting with zesty upbeat zing – as shrill and resonant as an opera diva belting out *Carmen* after sucking on a helium balloon. With Britain's marginal wine climate, these beautiful bubbles represent a new frontier in fine wine. And they belong inside your face.

Of course, sparkling wine is produced the world over, from the USA to Australia, South Africa to New Zealand. These wines can be noteworthy; just remember to look for any of these key phrases on the label to get the prime bottling that's had the royal treatment:

Traditional Method
Méthode Traditionelle
Klassische Flaschengärung
Cap Classique
Totes Amazeballs Bubbly

Well, perhaps the last one is made up, but it does raise the thorny issue of wine labels and why they are generally written in gobble-degook. Put bluntly, wine labels can be appallingly bad at communicating information as to what the fermented grape juice inside the bottle will actually taste like. Even the ones written in plain English can beguilingly promise that it will go with chicken, prawns, beef, apple pie and Monster Munch. But help is at hand; with a few anchor words in your drinks locker, predicting the quality and flavour of your bubbly can be made infinitely easier. Two words that you, Sir Chap, need to memorise, if only to ensure you remain on speaking terms with your wallet, is …

CRÉMANT (pronounced 'krem-on' without saying the final 't'). Crémant is bubbly made using the Champagne Method anywhere in France that's outside the Champagne region itself. Limoux down south is a hotspot, but you can also find it in Burgundy, the Loire and even Alsace. Grape varieties vary according to the region, but it's generally a good bet for bargain bubbles with a high degree of finesse. The sort of thing you'd consider uncorking to toast the butler in the morning for polishing your shoes particularly well. Learn the word, hunt it and sip it, if not constantly then whenever bubbles are required without selling the silverware.

FRANCIACORTA (pronounced 'fran-chee-a-korta'). Franciacorta is Italy's answer to champagne, made by the Traditional Method in the Franciacorta wine region north of Milan. An ancient Alpine glacier carved out an amphitheatre of moraine, and a funnel effect was added by God, ensuring that gentle breezes off the Italian lakes keep the vineyards fresh. Chardonnay, Pinot Noir and Pinot Blanc are the grapes, Satèn is a *blanc de blancs* (meaning it is made with only white grapes; the name refers to the satin texture of the drink), Brut is aged for a minimum of 18 months, with Satèn and Rosé aged for 24 months, Vintage 37 months and Riserva 60 months. Great with smoked salmon but sublime with goat's cheese drizzled with runny honey. Or just glug it with buttery pasta lavished with freshly chopped herbs.

THE NOBLE ART OF SABRAGE

Sabrage, from the word 'sabre', is the impressive trick of opening a bottle using a sword. It's as simple as a backhand in Ping Pong and, in fact, requires pretty much the same motion of the hand. Said to have originated when Mme Barbe-Nicole Ponsardin (more commonly known as Veuve Clicquot, the 'grande dame' of champagne) gave bottles to officers on horseback during the Napoleonic Wars, who used their swords to open the bottles while riding away to glory. We do not recommend attempting this without the proper tuition.

STEP 1: Only attempt on top-quality sparkling wine, whose bottles are robust enough. Champagne or English sparkling wine are your best bet.

STEP 2: Remove the foil and cage from the cork.

STEP 3: Find the seam on the bottle.

STEP 4: Grasp the base of the bottle and be careful of fingers.

STEP 5: Run your blade flat against the seam up to the lip of the glass below the cork and strike with the same fluidity as a backhand in Ping Pong.

The top of the bottle and the cork will fly away and you can serve the fizz. Be very careful, never attempt when drunk and do not forget that the top of the bottle becomes razor sharp, so no drinking from the bottle, however mad you are.

JAMES BOND *In the films, Bond is famed for his appreciation of Bollinger champagne. Olly was once invited to a Bond and Bollinger lunch in the Jules Verne restaurant, halfway up the Eiffel Tower, with Barbara Broccoli, the producer of the Bond films, and several other international wine critics of note. After lunch, a bottle was served 'blind' and the assembled winos were asked to correctly identify the vintage. Olly was the only man to pick it – 1975 Bollinger R.D. How did he know? In* A View To A Kill *Sir Roger Moore as 007 is served the exact same wine in the same restaurant halfway up the Eiffel Tower, which he sniffs and correctly identifies, to his dining companion's delight: 'I see you are a connoisseur, Monsieur Bond'. Nothing more needs to be said.*

QUOTES ON FIZZ

CHURCHILL: 'Remember gentlemen, it's not just France we are fighting for, it's champagne.'

SIR KINGSLEY AMIS: 'Best of all on its own, I have heard its admirers say, about 11.30 a.m., with a dry biscuit. Which leaves plenty of time to sneak out to the bar for a real drink.'

SIR ROGER MOORE, *The Spy Who Loved Me*: 'Maybe I misjudged Stromberg. Any man who drinks Dom Pérignon '52 can't be all bad.'

SIR SEAN CONNERY, *Goldfinger*: 'My dear girl, there are some things that just aren't done, such as drinking Dom Pérignon '53 above the temperature of 38 degrees Fahrenheit. That's just as bad as listening to the Beatles without earmuffs!'

SAMUEL JOHNSON: 'The feeling of friendship is like that of being comfortably filled with roast beef; love, like being enlivened with champagne.'

BETTE DAVIS (as Kit Marlowe in *Old Acquaintance*) 'There comes a time in every woman's life when the only thing that helps is a glass of champagne.'

DOROTHY PARKER 'Three be the things I shall never attain: Envy, content, and sufficient champagne.'

OLIVIA DE HAVILAND 'I would prefer to live forever in perfect health, but if I must at some time leave this life, I would like to do so ensconced on a chaise longue, perfumed, wearing a velvet robe and pearl earrings, with a flute of champagne beside me and having just discovered the answer to the last problem in a British cryptic crossword.'

ISADORA DUNCAN 'Before I was born my mother was in great agony of spirit and in a tragic situation. She could take no food except iced oysters and champagne. If people ask me when I began to dance, I reply, in my mother's womb, probably as a result of the oysters and champagne, the food of Aphrodite.'

MADAME LILY BOLLINGER 'I drink it when I'm happy and when I'm sad. Sometimes I drink it when I'm alone. When I have company I consider it obligatory. I trifle with it if I'm not hungry and drink it when I am. Otherwise, I never touch it – unless I'm thirsty.'

fashionable once more and, just like Victoria's lengthy reign, seems to be hell-bent on hanging around for an awfully long time to come. Having said the wine is rarely oaked, some producers are experimenting, such as La Violetta's Das Sakrileg 2014 Riesling from the wonderfully named region of Porongurup, Down Under, which the label boasts is 'Pure Riesling. Barrel fermented. Unfined, unfiltered. Pure sacrilege.' And as Olly put it after sampling a glass or two, 'Pluck my nostrils, that there is the power of love in a single splendid sip.'

SAUVIGNON BLANC: WILLIAM THE CONQUEROR.
Sauvignon Blanc is an unstoppable force. With its pedigree in French appellations such as Sancerre and Pouilly-Fumé on the upper reaches of the Loire, its razor-sharp refreshment and classy bright verve is a fan-winner and heart-and-mind conqueror par excellence. But its southern hemisphere incarnation in the outpost of Marlborough in New Zealand has sent it even further into the high street where it has penetrated all but the non-wine drinkers of the land. Made Kiwi style, its passion-fruit tropical sunshine-in-a-glass appeal sees it poured from the salons of subtlety to the nightclubs of naughtiness nationwide. Is it vulgar? Not really. It's a grape whose Loire heritage deserves respect. But, like William, its reign cannot last forever. Inevitably we shall tire of its dominance and with obscenities and gimmicks such as sparkling Sauvignon Blanc degrading it from the edges, the legacy of Sauvignon Blanc may well be extended by the more restrained styles coming from South Africa and Chile. Canny chaps will find it blended in white Bordeaux where it creates good snappy simple whites as well as complex and even oaked examples that remain hidden gems. Back on the Loire, Touraine Sauvignon Blanc can be good value but we'd also steer you towards Sauvignon Gris, especially from Chile, for a richer incarnation of a similarly zesty drink. And if it comes at you aiming a bow and arrow, duck or wear an armoured eye-patch.

CHENIN BLANC: GEORGE III. Chenin Blanc the chameleon is King George III: capable of austerity, effervescence and sweetly sharp madness. Its heartland is France's verdant Loire Valley where you can find it in appellations such as Vouvray which creates wines from dry to sweet – look for Sec, Demi-Sec, Moëlleux and Doux on the label. 'Savennières' is famous for making a dry style that feels like drinking wine through a suit of armour and needs years to soften in the bottle before attempting to suck it into your face. 'Bonnezeaux' is a famous and glorious sweet wine appellation with a wonderful name that sounds

marvellously like a dog biscuit. And Chenin even makes sparkling wines in appellations such as Crémant de Loire, Saumur and Montlouis. It's a riddle of a grape, but the headline flavour in almost all of its incarnations is similar to a Golden Delicious apple, perfectly poised with vibrant fruit and keen acidity. In South Africa it's become a poster boy for their sunny climate. Made in a fleshy dry or off-dry style, with gentle aromatics and a glossy texture it's a fine contender for spicy dishes and curries. And just like age ogre George III it's constantly being re-evaluated with plantings emerging in Sicily, New Zealand and elsewhere around the globe.

PINOT GRIGIO: EDWARD VI. Poor old Edward. With a dad whose personality could eclipse the very stars of supremacy, Edward was weak and rather unmemorable. Not his fault of course, being a youngster and suffering poor health and an early demise, but it does mean that, rather like Pinot Grigio, his character feels oddly neutral and hard to get truly excited about. Which makes it on the surface, astonishing that such a watery and dull grape variety has managed to march for glory across the palates of so many citizens. Or rather, perhaps it's because of its very inoffensiveness that it has been triumphant. No doubt there will come a time for Edward, sooner or later a biography is bound to unleash the true splendour of how he invented the internet centuries before computers and how he carved the format for *Top Gear* into the altar at Canterbury Cathedral. But until then, he is totally Pinot Grigio and a bit like Holland, generally flat. That said, spend a few quid on a Pinot Grigio from northern Italy and you may find something more dynamic than just the taste of Evian pass your lips. If it's Italian whites you're after, set your sails for the more flavoursome and characterful bottles from grapes such as Grechetto, Grillo, Fiano, Falanghina and Verdicchio dei Castelli di Jesi. Or just drink water – a pint of water with a capful of vodka stirred into it. For a richer wine that pairs supremely with spicy cooking, French Pinot Gris can be wonderful – Alsace examples tend to be rich, fruity and fat or, for a contemporary style that buzzes like an electric peach, Pinot Gris from New Zealand is arrestingly flavoursome. It's the same grape as Pinot Grigio, just riper on the vine and made in a fleshier and fruitier style. A bit like Edward VI in a parallel universe where he's a bearded Michael Flatley of a monarch, riding a horse bareback and merrily bonking his way through the courts of Europe.

VIOGNIER: KING JOHN. King John is said to have snuffed it thanks to a surfeit of peaches. Easily done, although had he blended apricots with peaches and gorged his way into eternity, he would really have been a lustful idolator of Viognier, for its precise flavour is as scented and soft as perfectly ripe peach romping with an apricot. Viognier is one of those grapes that chaps instinctively fear for its vulgarity. This is baseless. Viognier can be noble in the hands of great winemakers such as Georges Vernay and it is also the heart of one of the world's – and France's – smallest wine appellations: Château-Grillet in the northern Rhône. Condrieu is the heartland of Viognier and on occasion can offer surprising value on restaurant wine lists. It is also the only wine to sip alongside turbot, the king of fish, and the two together forge an alliance that not even the ruler of the Rumpus himself, Bacchus, could ever hope to cast asunder. As a white wine it's scented aromatics pair resplendently with gingery dishes (stir-friers take note), but it can also be co-fermented and blended with the mighty black grape Syrah (aka Shiraz) to make the scented reds of the northern Rhône that are found in Côte-Rôtie. The recipe has travelled far and wide throughout the world, the distinctive white grape adding an irresistible aromatic depth to these powerful red wines.

GRÜNER VELTLINER: THE HOUSE OF WINDSOR.

It's basically a bit German. Well, OK Grüner is Austrian, so actually not German at all. And neither are the Windsors. Phew, glad we got that straightened out. Grüner Veltliner tends to be as pristine and polished as an Alp buffed by a giant godly Jeeves. It has a curious subtle spicing that some people find reminds them of a gentle niff of white pepper, others find it more like cress. It's usually dry and with a certain richness of texture though it can be made into far plumper and even sweeter styles. A dry Grüner is generally unoaked and glorious to pair with shellfish such as scallops. It's also a superb match with tricky flavours such as asparagus and artichokes, which are traditionally regarded as wine slayers.

ALBARIÑO: CHARLES II. A bit of a dandy who loves a good time, Albariño benefits from a bit of discipline to bring out its zesty and nectarine-like bite. When allowed to run to flab it can be a disappointment but when it harnesses the fresh Atlantic verdant coastline of its home in north-western Spain, this Galician grape is capable of as much invigoration as braying nude into the Bay of Biscay like a wild saturnine ape. And it's a top-notch pairing with shellfish.

That's by no means the exhaustive list of white grapes. There's Italy's Renaissance Prince of Soave and a whole host of highly characterful varieties that Olly likes to call 'Pervert's Delight' such as bold, peachy Rhône whites from Marsanne to Roussanne, rose-scented Argentinian Torrontes, turbo-citrus Greek Assyrtiko, freshly delicate Portuguese Siria, nimble, delicate Japanese Koshu, white Rioja made with Viura, Tempranillo Blanco, Garnacha Blanca, Malvasia and more which creates wines in all shapes and sizes from fat and oaky to light and piercing, and Hungarian Furmint – a restrained kaleidoscope of exquisite aromatics. Not forgetting Basque Txakoli, as cutting as a grapefruit wielding a switchblade and as razor-edged as the Basque poet Gabriel Aresti's stinging exclamations. As for Semillon, it's an extraordinary grape making charged citrus whites when young that transform in the bottle over many years into flavours that can be surprisingly rich and nutty. And of course Semillon is also one of the blending grapes found in sweet Sauternes. Which presents the perfect moment to turn to the old classics that go by name rather than grape which every chap should learn, memorise and also get his chops round regularly.

VINHO VERDE: Portugal's biggest appellation in the north west, which specialises in producing white wines that are lightning sharp in their snappy dazzlement. A blend of local grapes including Loureiro, Arinto, Alvarinho and more, it's a brilliantly crisp summer quencher with a general spritz thanks to bottling with a touch of CO_2 to preserve freshness. With alcohol levels hovering around 11 per cent, it's also a winning bottle to crack open if the afternoon requires retaining a modicum of mental freshness. Reds and sparkling wines can also be found but we reckon the key to Vinho Verde's good value and appeal is that it remains curiously unfashionable. Despite this, the wine remains surprisingly decent and is well worth revisiting.

'White wine is like electricity. Red wine looks and tastes like a liquefied beefsteak.' JAMES JOYCE

MUSCADET: A bit like Casablanca, you forget how good it is until it's happening to your face. Muscadet is the place, the wine and the grape. The best examples are Muscadet de Sèvre et Maine Sur Lie, the 'Sur Lie' indicating that the wine has been aged on the lees (spent yeast cells), which fleshes out texture and imparts a discreetly savoury moreish character that can, in extreme circumstances, lead to spontaneous singing. Olly was once removed from a taxi in downtown Nantes, unofficial capital of the Muscadet vineyards, for exploding into a rendition of Frankie Goes To Hollywood's 'The Power of Love' after a particularly fine shellfish and Muscadet themed feast. Of course oysters and Muscadet belong in the same mouthful, but another contender for a wine named famously after a place rather than a grape is, of course … SOUND THE TRUMP … .

SIR KINGSLEY SAYS *'Nothing Spanish, because too horrible; nothing Yugoslav, because too boring; nothing French, because too expensive, and often horrible as well.'*

CHABLIS: Yes, dear old Chablis. It's Chardonnay. Fact. Generally unoaked but sometimes winemakers have been known to dabble. Straight Chablis is OK. Petit Chablis can be good value. But look for Premier Cru on the label, which in the best examples feels like sipping stardust such is the alluring and dazzling lasting trail of glittering freshness that tantalises for an aeon after every sip. Grand Cru Chablis are even bolder and richer and can age happily for many years in bottle but they cost a fair old whack so make sure you're the guest of a well-heeled aunt before you order a couple of bottles to suck down with your luncheon. These Premier and Grand Cru sites are named and favoured south-facing sites with the best conditions for creating wines of wonder. Their names and characteristics are unique and the very best way to get to know them is to pop over and do some gentle strolling or cycling around the place. The same goes for the famous names of Bourgogne (Burgundy) further south such as Meursault, Puligny-Montrachet and St-Aubin. Just go there, wander about and try some contrasting styles. Their origin is as important as the grape along with the winemaker and it's a question of licking a wealth of bottles to unlock the truth inside you. Every bottle of wine is a vortex of opinion.

INSATIABLE ALSATIANS

If white wine is your thing, then by all means rummage in France's Burgundy for the big names, or revel in New Zealand Sauvignon Blanc for your fruity thrills, but please direct your taste buds to target and lock on to an oft-overlooked region that excels at creating fine whites of splendour that really ought to be more pricey than they are. Alsace appellation contrôlée is your straightforward wine – it's OK and accounts for a huge proportion of production – but chaps need to aim higher: Alsace Grand Cru. These are individual vineyards with near-magic powers to create white wines of huge character and stunning intensity. The problem is telling whether it's dry, off dry or even sweeter than that. Some makers give an indication on the bottle, but the truth is, you're going to have to taste it to really know. Just remember that, for these Grand Cru sites, the winemaker is trying to channel the spirit of the place and the year, so if it's fruitier than you were

---

'OAK' IS NOT A SWEAR WORD *Contrary to what you may have overheard in the salons of society and around the dinner tables of disquietude, oak is not a swear word. When a white wine is aged in oak barrels the wood adds texture and flavour. Subtlety is key, just as salt and pepper in the hands of a great chef, or a delicate frame around a work of art enhances the overall composition, so oak can boost a wine. It benefits many Chardonnay wines, including most white Burgundy – as well as top-drawer red wines – but other white grapes such as Sauvignon, Riesling, Gewurztraminer are generally happier unoaked. Of course, in the wrong hands the flavour from oak can make a white wine taste like sweet vanilla wee wee, in which case swearing is 100% appropriate. Gustav usually opts for 'Great Scott man, this wine is Satan's sample' before hurling the glass and bottle in the fireplace and challenging the waiter to a duel.*

---

expecting, then embrace it and let yourself be carried by the generous conditions that have made their way to you from the open skies of a few short months via the bottle. The three big grapes in Alsace are Riesling, Gewurztraminer and Pinot Blanc. **Riesling,** which can have real verve in Alsace in bottles such as Cuvée Frédéric Emile from Trimbach, a blend of Riesling from two Grand Cru sites, Geisberg and Osterberg – it's sublimely zesty when young and ages beautifully into a richer, broader even toasty incarnation; altogether a mesmeric white wine. **Pinot Gris** can be rich and peachy and its flavours and aromas can remind you of a pear mating with a quince. **Gewurztraminer** (the Alsatians omit the umlaut) is like sipping a rose bush scattered with lychees and will appeal to fans of Turkish Delight; **Muscat** has an orangey-tinged scent to it and **Pinot Blanc** is your best bet for simple invigorating and most likely dry stuff from the region. **Sylvaner** creates wines that are similarly racy and fresh but planting is in decline. We've listed the grapes because Alsace wines indicate them on the label, unlike most of France. If you spot *Vendange Tardive*, it's a late-harvest wine that's going to be relatively sweet, while a *Sélection de Grains Nobles* will always be sweet and only occurs in amazing vintages when the conditions are perfect for the 'noble rot' to intensify both the sweetness and acidity in the grapes. These wines are chap nirvana and should be sipped sparingly when revitalisation of the soul is required. Crémant d'Alsace, the local bubbly, is well worth looking out for – and you should visit this enchanting region, sheltered to the west by the Vosges Mountains and stretching away towards the Rhine in the east, as it is one of the world's most quaint and charming wine spots.

MATCHING FOOD WITH WHITE WINE

CEVICHE: Sauvignon Blanc or Torrontes.

CRAB: Viognier or for more delicate dishes, Greek Malagousia.

CURRY: Huge range of flavours to consider but for a basic introduction, experiment with Pinot Gris for a decent all-round white, Chenin Blanc also fun and for an aromatic assault Gewurztraminer is a whale of unstoppable scented force.

GOAT'S CHEESE: Sauvignon Blanc, no brainer.

LOBSTER: Champagne or English sparkling wine.

MOZZARELLA: Prosecco. Do it.

OYSTERS: Muscadet, Chablis, Champagne, English bubbly.

ROAST PORK: Oaky Chardonnay or one of the rich blends of grapes from France's Rhône such as Marsanne and Roussanne.

SCALLOPS: Grüner Veltliner. They flipping love one another.

TURBOT: Viognier. King of fish bellows 'Arise, Sir Wine and rub yourself into my back.' Not literally, just drink it alongside the dish. Scrummy.

VANILLA ICE CREAM: Pour sweet Pedro Ximenez over it and revel in its glossy black splendour. A white grape, but a deep treacle of a wine that engenders the desire to cuddle almost instantly. Stand well back.

WHAT IS ROSÉ?

All colour in wine comes from the grape skins – juice macerating. Rosé is simply the result of the juice spending less time on skins, either bled off from a red wine fermentation in the *saignée*, or made as a rosé in its own right with a small amount of skin contact. A third method is to blend red and white wine, but in practice this is rare and only really occurs in the Champagne region.

TOP PINK CHAMPAGNE includes: Lanson NV, Bollinger Grande Année or Dom Pérignon for a very special occasion.

TOP ENGLISH PINK SPARKLING WINES include Camel Valley from Cornwall and Wiston from West Sussex.

And you can find good-value pink cava – 'rosado' - from Spain. For still rosé, which you can find all over the world, as a vague indicator, the darker the colour the fuller the flavour; that said, you can find pale 'blush' rosé from the USA, which is intensely – if not horribly – sweet. For this reason, the rosé that every chap should quaff come summer is the stuff from Provence. Bandol is a particularly superior appellation and can even create rosés that are capable of ageing.

MATEUS ROSÉ Favoured by the Queen, Jimi Hendrix and, er, Saddam Hussein, this pink from Portugal is something of a throwback to times gone by and more of a reminder of pink's enduring popularity. Chaps only drink it in private.

REGARDING ROSÉ *Pink is not girly. In fact, pink is for everyone, chaps included. Most chaps would have no problem sipping pink fizz on a summer lawn during a picnic with fellow chaps, so it comes as something of a surprise to both Gustav and Olly that a question mark still hovers over pink drinks. The reality is that, where rosé once stood for a few big brand names that were rather sweet and unenthralling, today rosé wine comes in all shapes and sizes and in fact in some cases is so butch it's practically red wine.*

DRESSING FOR DRINK

In order to benefit from the subtleties of this oft-overlooked member of your armoury of alcohol, one should always slightly overdress for the occasion. Wear a very lightweight bespoke suit from Savile Row, made from the sheerest worsted money can buy. Ensure it is double breasted and that the lapels nearly reach the shoulder seams, and pair it with a pair of Goodyear-welted co-respondents that have been polished within an inch of their short lives. In the breast pocket, an exquisite pocket square made from some rare Japanese silk, which you may occasionally withdraw in order to wipe away the tears induced by a particularly sublime Gewuztraminer.

LEGENDS OF LIBATION
Sir Kingsley Amis

The sommelier showed him the wine list, murmuring a benediction in French. 'I'll have the Graves', Kingsley told him, pronounced (wrongly and deliberately) to rhyme with 'waves'. Lifting his glass, he sniffed, tasted, and spat the wine on the table. 'Very good,' he said.

Thus would one have encountered legendary soak, author and ladies' man Sir Kingsley Amis (probably, though not necessarily, before he was knighted). The craft of writing he learned at Oxford, where he had miraculously arrived after being sired an only child by a clerk for Colman's Mustard, and at the typewriter that he never failed to approach every single morning, despite daily hangovers. The craft of drinking he learned also at Oxford, but later honed his skills by taking his lunch at the Garrick Club, where the food was a brief interruption to the drinking.

Kingsley (AKA the Kingster, or simply 'The King') had his own set of club rules, all of which had to be obeyed by anyone in his circle. The first was never to sit to lunch until at least two pre-prandial drinks had been consumed. He devoted a long passage in his memoirs to an obscure man from his past, whose principal impression on Amis was to have made rather meanly sized Bloody Marys. The second Rule of Kingsley regarded bores, who Kingsley would eliminate by barking, 'Z, over here' from the bar, referring to his chum Ronald Zeegen, who would leap over to save the conversation.

Wherever he was in the world, Kingsley would maintain a prodigious intake of alcohol. On a long drive across Mexico in the 1960s, he packed the car with enough provisions in a large basket to mix all the passengers a cocktail at precisely 11.30 every morning. His favourite serving was a 'Fake Negroni', made with gin, Campari and tonic. Trips to the cinema in London were equally lubricated; from his pockets Kingsley would produce miniatures of gin and bottles of tonic and even a sliced lemon, handing round G&Ts to his companions.

A typical lunch for Kingsley would commence with two dry martinis while he considered the menu; a bottle of Chablis Grand Cru with the first course; a bottle of Château Lafite-Rothschild with the second; a glass of Sauternes with pudding, a port with the cheese and a large Calvados to round off. Was Kingsley an alcoholic? Journalist Rosie Boycott, his lunch companion for two years, thinks not: 'There's something about people who can get to that age and can drink. That they've survived and they're still tottering along probably means that the alcohol is not quite as destructive to them as it is to younger people.' Sir Kingsley's own definition of an alcoholic was simply someone who drank alone, something he never once did in his life.

Despite becoming unbearably curmudgeonly in old age, there was a joie de vivre to Kingsley's imbibing. There was no better way for people to get to know each other than from 'ceasing to be sober together', as he put it. Drink, drinkers and drinking formed a large part of Amis's fiction too, with at least one big boozer in every one of his 25 novels. Here are the thoughts of Maurice Allington in *The Green Man*: *'I was drunk, in fact drunk with that pristine freshness, that semi-mystical elevation of spirit which, every time, seems destined to last for ever. There was nothing worth knowing that I did not know, or rather would not turn out to know when I saw my way to turning my attention to it.'*

CHAPTER 4

RED WINE

Pugilists of Faith

To make red wine you need to be a person of dreams, skill and wide-eyed wonderment, but the biggest talent of all that you'll need is to be able to tell the future with your tongue. Making red wine, you see, is an extraordinary act of faith. In essence, the winegrower is in a perpetual high stakes face-off with the weather in any given year, with every grape, bunch and shoot that fails to deliver leaving a potential hole in the coffers. The conditions of any vintage loom over the winemaker like a thunderous boxer sent from the shadows of Rocky Balboa's very stubble, to instil a sense of devotion and respect for the land and fruit placed in the winery's tender care. In 2012, for example, the weather was so damp across our home shores that many UK vineyards simply didn't get a crop. That means going to work every day for a year and taking home zero pay. Thankfully, 2014 was a bumper year. Phew.

To mitigate the risk of the weather giving your vineyard a proper roughing over, wine-growers over the centuries have learned to plant different varieties of grapes in plots side by side that ripen at different times. This gives rise to blending of grapes, which gives the unique character and flavour to the wines of a particular region – for example Bordeaux, where Cabernet Sauvignon and Merlot are often intertwined.

But before we talk about the different grape varieties, let's look at how winemakers inform us as to the contents of their seductive green bottles. While perusing the shelves of your local supermarket, off-licence or wine merchant, you may notice that some wines advertise their grape, while others their region or vineyard. Why is this? In Europe, historically there's been a tendency to label wines by the place they come from, for example, Volnay in France (made from Pinot Noir), Barolo in Italy (Nebbiolo grape) and Rioja in Spain (a blend of red grapes headlined by Tempranillo). When the 'New World' winemaking revolution took off, naming the grape variety and talking about its qualities in plain English reinvigorated wine labels by being both simple and useful. Europe is cottoning on to this and using the back label to give clearer information to some degree, but part of the infuriating charm of wine is that, to learn about flavour, you have to arrive via geography, with a brief stopover at history and an additional module of learning every European language there is.

How is a non-wine connoisseur supposed to know which grape varieties are in a wine that simply says, for example, Côtes du Roussillon on the label? It's one of those stubborn mysteries of wine that certain places believe they are the apotheosis of certain grapes and assume it's commonly known what goes into the wine – such as Chablis, which is made from Chardonnay, or champagne, which is often a blend of Chardonnay, Pinot Noir and Pinot Meunier. Côtes du Roussillon is a vast wine-growing region of southern France where the tangy Carignan grape is big news, working well in blends more than as a solo act, except for wines made from old bush vines with top-quality fruit. The devastating truth is that, for European wines, unless the winemaker has helpfully listed the grape varieties on the back label or written a cogent tasting note such as 'light and elegant' or 'rich and spicy', you're more or less in the swim and only a personal visit to every single vineyard in Europe will enlighten you.

'There is no such thing as a bad Côtes du Rhone,' trumpet so-called experts from the saloon bars of pubs across the land. However, there's a grain of truth in what they say. Côtes du Rhône roughly translates into English as 'the hills of the Rhône', a region stretching over 100 miles from Lyon to Avignon, where many red grape varieties flourish, led by Grenache, Syrah, Mourvèdre and Carignan, all of which give robust qualities to this gluggable wine with a warming hearty twist. The key to the region's reliability comes from blending these red grapes together. So even in a patchy vintage with these grapes ripening at different times, the wine grower has an insurance policy against total disaster. Our tip is to look for 'Côtes du Rhône Villages' on the label, which is a step up in quality from the basic Côtes du Rhône for not much more cash. And in excellent vintages such as 2009 and 2010, these bottles punch well above their price point on the UK wine shelves.

Which leads us to the age-old question as to whether a bad year from a good vineyard is better than a good year from a bad vineyard. There's a saying among winemakers that 'you can't make good wine from bad grapes' so one route to happy sipping in poor vintages is to follow the quality of a winery and the pedigree of the vineyard. Even if the wine from a bad year is less mighty than a good vintage, it ought to be comparatively better value and represent the winery's best efforts in challenging conditions. Or better yet, have a glance at the many 'vintage charts' online and steer your course accordingly. Beaujolais, for example, had top vintages in 2009, 2010 and 2013 (forget Nouveau, select from the ten named 'Cru' offerings from places such as

Morgon and Fleurie) and scout those wines, especially on restaurant wine lists, where choosing a good year for a few quid more will significantly improve the feast.

One of the most baffling and risky situations a chap in need of wine may find himself in is at that bastion of blandness, the corner shop, with a tenner burning a hole in his pocket and a thirsty lady waiting in a taxi. Luckily, corner shops have got better at stocking wine and reining in the prices, but the big issue is how long that bottle has been on the shelf, quietly baking in direct sunlight, rendering its contents more like soup than splendour. The sensible chap uses his honed jungle logic to select wine based on a combination of reliable quality and decent turnover of bottles – and that invariably means sourcing from a big brand. Some can be trusted to deliver the goods at this kind of level: from New Zealand, sound the trump for Brancott Estate; from Australia thump your tub for Jacob's Creek; from Chile toot the trombone for Casillero del Diablo; and from Spain clack your castanets for Campo Viejo Rioja. You can even find French brands with significant distribution, such as the wines of Paul Mas, which are generally splendid. These wines may not blow sparks up your trumpet but they will deliver a decent enough glug in your hour of need.

When it comes to national viticultural superiority, it has always been assumed that the French still lead the way. These days, it can safely be said that no single country is overall the best wine producer, with various pockets all producing top notch vino, but the French can certainly still claim to be the cradle of wine. Where France is winning new fans is with fruity wines from the sunny south, where the canny chap should hunt for bargains. Appellations such as St-Chinian, Faugères and Pic-St-Loup offer quality and value. The diversity of France remains tough for other countries to compete with, and it deserves respect and praise for heralding wine from the past into a global future. On no account should you reject the stuff at the lower end of the market, either. Sometimes a Vin de France or Vin de Pays (the French equivalent to the European IGP Indication Géographique Protégée) can be a surprise hit. There are plenty of excellent winemakers who disobey the rules of their appellation, by chosing which grape varieties to plant or by defiantly using a screw cap instead of a cork; both of which might oblige them to label their wine with a more humble Vin de Pays or IGP categorisation.

Another popular myth hovering around the mind of our putative off-licence located chap is that New World wines are all a bit on the strong side, with occasional sightings of 14.5%, compared to the traditional 11% for French and Spanish wines. There is a reason for this beyond wanting us to get terribly drunk, and it is because New World wines come from hot places – heat produces sugar in the fruit which converts to alcohol. Many New World producers are getting better at where they plant their vines, how they orient their vineyards and what specific varieties of grapes they grow, as well as using techniques in the winery to keep alcohol levels more successfully under control. Mornington Peninsula in Australia, for example, makes surprisingly fine wine and there are pockets of California, such as Russian River, where elegant styles of Pinot Noir are being produced. Oregon Pinot Noir has some outstanding producers from J. Christopher Wines to Eyrie Vineyards.

THE CHAP'S GUIDE TO THE GLORY OF GRAPES

——————//——————

CABERNET SAUVIGNON: The Prime Minister, thick skinned and powerful. Cabernet's spiritual heartland is Bordeaux, where it is principally blended with Merlot to soften its enduring toughness. In youth it's like a blackcurrant wearing a leather jacket. It's a grape that's built to age and, as the months and years go by, its wines soften and become more savoury. Other notable places to sample Cabernet Sauvignon include Coonawarra in Australia, where the wines are laden with deep fragrant fruit and a curious minty whiff, thanks to the local eucalyptus trees, which are said to imbue the very breeze with their magical minty oils.

MERLOT: The Fleshy Tailor, perfectly cut to smooth out the rhino horn of Cabernet Sauvignon's thrust. Merlot is as ubiquitous as mothballs, fizzy drinks and games of football. It's a friendlier grape than Cabernet Sauvignon, in that it's easier to ripen and tastes softer and mellower. On the right bank of the Garonne in Bordeaux, it's the headline act in some of the world's most expensive and famous reds, such as Petrus, and it's also blended with Cabernet Franc in such illustrious bottles as Cheval Blanc. In Chile, Carmenère was for a long time mistaken for Merlot, so that, even today, if you ask for 'Merlot' in Chile, you might end up with Carmenère. For a real glass of Merlot, you need to request 'Merlot-Merlot'.

CABERNET FRANC: The Aesthete. Cabernet Franc may not be as famous as its offspring Cabernet Sauvignon, but it exudes understated class and sophistication. Cabernet Franc is significantly lighter and more elegant than a beefy glass of Cabernet Sauvignon, so much so that lighter examples from France's Loire especially lend themselves to chilling in the summer months. Look out for names like Chinon and Bourgeuil, along with Saumur Champigny, which often yields startling aromas astonishingly close to pencil shavings. Also found as part of the blending mix in Bordeaux, there are tremendous examples around the world such as Bruwer Raats' work in South Africa, Pulenta Estate in Argentina, Jamsheed's Ma Petite Francine in Australia and O Fournier's Alfa Centauri and Urban Maule blends sourced from Chile.

MALBEC: The Circus Strongman. A simple motto to remember for one of the world's simplest food and drink pairings is 'Meat with Malbec'. Malbec tends to be hefty and you certainly wouldn't want it to become enraged with you. Malbec's passport seems to be most heavily stamped in Argentina, where it has become the emblem of big-hearted powerful reds, perfect to deploy with sirloin steak. Also known as 'Cot', Malbec is again one of the Bordeaux brigade, but also found in the southwestern French haven of Cahors, with its famous 'black wine'. It is the kind of wine that Brian Blessed would probably enjoy drinking to celebrate conquering Everest, or to toast the annual migration of his beard as it takes flight to the Hidden Kingdom of Hair.

PINOT NOIR: The Dandy, prone to nimble flights of fancy. Pinot Noir pays deference to no-one but its own mysterious vagaries. As ethereal as an elf riding an angel to a pixie convention, it is among the most elegant and whimsical red wines. When Pinot Noir is cheap, it can be as rude as a motorcycle in a swimming pool. But when harnessed to the ideal vintage conditions – not too hot, not too wet – and, crucially, in the hands of the right winemaker, it can be beguiling, surreptitious and mesmeric in its capacity to age and unfold secret scents and hidden flavours. For bargains, Romania is the future; for herby depth Otago in New Zealand is your place (top producers include Rippon, Valli, Burn Cottage, Felton Road and Two Paddocks) but for expensive wines that reflect their vintages like a mirror, Burgundy remains the apotheosis from the sacred places of La Tâche and Volnay to Nuits-St-Georges and Gevrey-Chambertin. Just make sure someone else is paying the bill before you order. The world's priciest wine, incidentally, is a Pinot Noir from the holy site of Burgundy's Domaine de la Romanée-Conti, which Olly has visited, revered and emerged victorious from, after a rigorous blind tasting in the hallowed cellars.

SHIRAZ: The Firebrand, thanks to its smoky wreath. Shiraz is the same grape as Syrah, with a fuller flavour and higher alcohol. Often this is determined by where it's planted – Syrah for cooler places and more elegant wines, Shiraz for hotter places with more of a fruit–booze detonation. Olly was once told by Australian viticulturist Steve Brunato that 'Shiraz grows like a bloody octopus' and he further confided after a glass or two that on occasion he felt sure he could almost hear it whispering in the vineyard. Hermitage in France's northern Rhône is considered the high point of this grape, but we'd direct you to the neighbouring appellations of Cornas and St-Joseph for jollies at marginally less crippling prices. Shiraz can also be part of a blend, as in Côtes du Rhône, but it reaches its boldest incarnation in Australian hotspots such as the Barossa Valley. The sunny south of France has some wonderful blends featuring this grape, including Pic-St-Loup, St-Chinian and Faugères, well worth your attention to save money as well as tantalise your taste buds.

TEMPRANILLO: The Backbencher. It's a not a name we hear often enough, but this age-worthy grape is the backbone of the famous red blend, which we all know as Rioja. Tempranillo means 'ripens early', and in northern Spain in the Rioja region it's blended with Garnacha (aka Grenache) and Mazuelo (aka Carignan), which is more or less the recipe for Rioja – that oaky-mellow easy-drinking Spanish red that every chap adores. There are three principal levels of Rioja: 'Crianza', aged in barrel and bottle for a minimum of one year each – spot on for some week-night lamb chops. 'Reserva', aged for at least two years in barrel and one year in bottle – Sunday lunch perfection. 'Gran Reserva', aged for a minimum of two years in barrel and three years in bottle and only made in the best years – great for a banquet, feast or private indulgence. The more Rioja is aged, the more savoury – and pricey – it becomes. If your favourite flavour is a fresh blackberry, drink reds young. If you're more of a mushroom man, go for aged earthy beauties.

NEBBIOLO: The Jockey because it appears light but in fact is very robust. Pale in colour, it is among the most tannic of grapes, and graces the world behind the name of the holy hillsides of northern Italy's Barolo. A wonder with richer meats and wildly irresistible in truffle season overlooking the Alps from the burnished vineyards of Barolo itself, this is a red wine that's a whole lot finer after a few years in the bottle to soften and settle.

HOW IS
RED WINE MADE?

———//———

The colour of red wine comes from the skins of the grapes. To demonstrate this for yourself, when devouring a succulent black table grape, keep the skin in your mouth and chomp it a few times between your front teeth before examining a dot of the juice on the end of your finger – it looks suspiciously like red wine. But before such humble grape juice can call itself wine, rather like Sherlock Holmes focusing his mind from the fuzz of opium into razorblade precision, there are many transformations that must flourish.

Not all grape skins are alike. Some have more pigment than others and certain grape skins are thicker than others – for example, Cabernet Sauvignon's tweed overcoat versus Pinot Noir's dandy silk scarf. This has an impact on the texture of the wine in your glass. Whatever their particular variety and quality, once wine grapes have been picked from the vineyard (either by hand or machine) they are quickly taken to the winery, where they are crushed and de-stemmed. Sometimes a technique called 'whole bunch fermentation' is deployed, which can give wines more silkiness, elegance and fragrance, as well as keeping alcohol levels from rampaging skywards. But, generally, stems are discarded and the grapes are gently squished, ready for the metamorphosis from fruit juice into the sip of the gods.

The skins, pips and pulp are tipped into a vat and are either left to macerate and gently extract colour at a low temperature, or sometimes 'thermo-vinified' at a higher temperature to give them a deeper colour. The crushed grapes tend to begin fermentation at around 20°C, when the yeast is warm enough to be coaxed into life and start converting sugar into alcohol. Sometimes a winemaker will use a yeast from a laboratory to enhance certain flavour and aroma characteristics, whereas some wine-growers (notably those who describe their wine as 'natural') prefer to leave their grapes to begin fermentation naturally with the 'wild yeast' that is present on the grapes in the vineyard – this may take a little longer to kick in and give less predictable results, but can contribute further to the wine's unique character.

Back in the vat, the pulp and skins of red fermenting wine rise to the surface and, to make sure of a decent colour extraction, winemakers either 'pump over' by sucking fermenting wine from the bottom and hosing it over the top of the cap of skins, or 'punching down' the cap with a paddle. Some winemakers choose to further concentrate their wine by drawing off some lightly coloured wine at this stage, which they can sell as rosé. The rest of the wine usually takes between one and three weeks to complete fermentation, when the yeast has converted all the remaining natural sugar into alcohol and conveniently snuffs it without a murmur, grumble or salary. The 'free run' wine is drawn off, while the remaining skins are gently pressed. A portion of this 'press wine' is blended with the free run wine. The wine-maker may then age his red wine in barrels to add further toasty and spicy flavours, as well as to enrich the texture; or he can bottle the wine unoaked to give a youthful fruity quality – the sort of red you'd sip with a late morning platter of charcuterie.

Filtering a wine can soften the texture, while unfiltered wines usually leave a bit of sediment from the skins – if you pour the wine carefully and slowly, you can easily catch the sediment in the shoulder of the bottle. Decanting with a wine filter is, of course, another option. We at Chap HQ advocate decanting all reds into a jug or decanter to unleash their full spectrum of aromas and flavours. The only exception is very old vintages of red wine, which are extremely delicate and require the same treatment as a revered octogenarian emperor carefully carried in a sedan chair, rather than being strapped into a rollercoaster and losing his toga, dignity, mind and bones.

WINE TERMINOLOGY

Wine terminology is as enervating as a politician trying not to admit that they've behaved in a duplicitous manner despite being caught red-handed. Take *terroir*. It's silly to use a French word, when our homegrown Master of Wine Tim Atkin suggests a perfectly serviceable English alternative: 'Somewhereness'. *Terroir* is simply shorthand for all the specific conditions surrounding the vine that influence the final wine – soil, climate, aspect, local traditions etc. Hardly rocket science. Here are some further decodings of wine gibberish:

LEGS: The tears of wine that trickle down the glass bowl once you've swirled a wine. Generally slower and thicker legs indicate a higher level of alcohol.

LENGTH: Refers to the amount of time the flavours of the wine linger on your palate once you've sipped it. Generally longer indicates better quality.

PRONOUNCED: Simply means powerful and can refer to the aroma or flavour of a wine.

TANNIN: Tannin comes from the grapes' skins and pips and is the stuff that dries your mouth out when you sip a full-bodied red. You'll experience a similar feeling if you sip an over-stewed cup of tea. Tannic reds need food with a robust texture, such as Cheddar cheese or steak, to soften their forceful structure.

There are plenty more, of course. We have come up with some brand new phrases and terms that we feel perfectly encapsulate the splendour of wine without resorting to words that feel as futile as shouting at a blackbird.

SCRUMPERLY: A wine that is properly scrumptious.

WART VORTEX: A glass that is utter filth – and not in a good way.

RE-BOOT: The perfect wine at the perfect moment to recalibrate one's sense of wonder.

TOO MUCH STARCH AROUND THE COLLAR: A wine with so much tannin that it feels as though you are chewing on a recently starched shirt.

ADEQUATE: Very good indeed.

SERVING RED WINE

Henry VIII, aside from being a massive show-off, was also determined to out-wine his French counterpart Francis I and built a fountain or two that spouted hundreds of gallons of free vino. A replica has been built at Hampton Court, which Olly has personally inspected and is planning to install a similar concept in his garden.

Thankfully, a chap does not require such an installation to attain optimum pleasure from his cheeky glass of red.

First of all, a note on decanting. Olly is a firm believer in decanting all wines (except fizz or very old reds) no matter how humble the liquid. Simply the very act of pouring and aerating the wine goes a long way to open up its aromas and flavour. The shape of the decanter is purely aesthetic and does nothing to alter the flavour. Any old jug will do, but a chap ought to have a range of decanters to suit the appropriate theatrics of a particular event. Their shapes include:

THE CLARET JUG: Tall and elegant.

THE SHIP'S DECANTER: Squat and designed to prevent spillage with the roll of the ship.

THE BOTTLE: A decanter uniquely designed by Olly to fit equally splendidly in the hand, on the table, in the fridge door and in the dishwasher.

As for glassware, the most appalling sin is a glass that tapers outwards, which will disperse aromas and steal pleasure from your very face. A decent wine glass should taper inwards and only ever be filled to the point of return, where the glass begins to turn back on itself. The best manufacturer, in our view, is Zalto, whose wine glasses belong in every chap's collection.

MATCHING FOOD WITH WINE

There is a lot of conjecture when it comes to pairing food and red wine. We are of the opinion that a chap should be guided by his palate rather than convention. Light red wines, for example, work brilliantly with meaty fish such as monkfish, swordfish and tuna steaks. And light red wines may be better served chilled rather than at room temperature. With certain meats, such as pork and chicken, you may be better off with an oaky white (see page 35) than a red. Olly was once served lobster in a red wine sauce with a Chianti, a pairing which on the surface would make Bacchus bite off his own toes with fright, but which in event turned out to be indisputably delicious. There are, nonetheless, a few guidelines to help you achieve maximum personal pleasure:

Generally the chunkier the texture of your grub, the heftier the wine should be.

Always match your wine to the boldest flavour in the dish, which may come from a sauce or dressing.

If you enjoy it, it's the best wine match in the world.

CHILLING RED WINE

Young fruity reds can be served chilled in summertime, including grapes such as Gamay and Pinot Noir. Bear in mind that in days gone by prior to central heating, room temperature would have been significantly cooler. For reds in general, 18°C is about right, but on a hot day in summer, consider plopping your bottle of French Saumur-Champigny or Italian Dolcetto d'Alba into an ice bucket and revel in its splendour. Such wines are also perfectly wonderful to pair with meaty fish from tuna to swordfish.

———

'Beer is made by men, wine by God.'
MARTIN LUTHER

———

CORKS V. SCREW TOPS

A few years back, the risk of cork taint was high, which gave screw caps the edge and made some ask whether it might be curtains for cork. But the cork industry has massively cleaned up its act. Today we'd still recommend screw caps for all sorts of wine from everyday supermarket plonk right through to fine wines to preserve flavour as the winemaker intended. Similarly, DIAM composite corks are also good and avoid cork taint. As for cork itself, it remains a good closure, allowing a certain amount of oxygen in before locking more or less like a stone – fantastic for gently ageing wines in a cellar. Just remember, if a bottle is sealed with a cork you need to store it on its side to prevent the cork drying out. If you are served a corked wine (it will smell musty, similar to damp cardboard) in a restaurant, insist on exchanging it for another bottle of the same, and if you bought it in a shop take it back and ask for an exchange of the same bottle. A corked wine is emphatically not a wine with bits of cork floating in your glass – just fish those out and carry on drinking with all the intent of a lion licking a zebra's face off.

MIXING RED WINE *Queen Victoria's favourite drink was supposedly a mix of claret and single malt whisky. We pledge to sample it as soon as we've recovered from the shock. Our experience of mixing red wine is inspired by Spain's red wine spritzer Tinto de Verano – equal parts cheap red wine and good-quality lemonade laced with chopped fruit and ice in a jug. Scrumperly.*

SIR KINGSLEY SAYS *'Hit your wine merchant across the mouth when, innocently, he recommends you to "buy for laying down". It is true that wine improves and increases in value with age, broadly speaking, and that you can save a lot of money by seeing to it that the ageing takes place after, rather than before, you buy it. But "Pay now, drink in 1984" strikes me as a dreadfully depressing slogan.'*

MARRIAGES MADE IN HEAVEN *Corbières, a spicy red from France's Languedoc region, rules the little sheep, thanks to a compound called thymol, which is generally present in both the wine and the meat. A match made in heaven. Though not for the lamb. Actually literally for the lamb, if there's a heaven for lambs. With roast pork, oaked white wines rather than the popular glass of red are actually splendid (apparently it's to do with a compound called vanillin, which is present in both) or if you're serving roast pork with lashings of apple sauce, a German Spätlese Riesling chimes beautifully.*

A SKULLFUL OF WINE

Lord Byron's favourite drinking vessel, when entertaining at Newstead Abbey, was a human skull. It had been found in the gardens of the former Augustinian abbey, as Byron himself explained: 'There had been found by the gardener, in digging, a skull that had probably belonged to some jolly monk or friar of the Abbey, about the time it was demonasteried. Observing it to be of giant size, and in a perfect state of preservation, a strange fancy seized me of having it set and mounted as a drinking cup. I accordingly sent it to town, and it returned with a very high polish and of a mottled colour like tortoiseshell.'

In homage to an ancient Gothic tradition, Byron founded the Order of the Skull, and would pass around the skull, filled with claret, to his guests. He wrote an ode to the skull, 'Lines Inscribed upon a Cup Formed from a Skull', which featured the lines:

Better to hold the sparkling grape,
Than nurse the earth-worm's slimy brood;
And circle in the goblet's shape

The drink of gods, than reptile's food.
Where once my wit, perchance, hath shone,
In aid of others' let me shine;
And when, alas! our brains are gone,
What nobler substitute than wine?

John Trelawney, friend to both Byron and Shelley, presided over the latter's cremation. Byron asked if he could keep the skull of his dead friend and Trelawney refused, knowing full well it would be converted into another macabre drinking vessel.

'Man being reasonable must get drunk;
The best of life is but intoxication;
Glory, the grape, love, gold – in these are sunk –
The hopes of all men and of every nation.'

CLARET *Claret is what the Brits often call red wine from Bordeaux. But the word itself refers back to when Bordeaux wines were paler in the Middle Ages, when it meant 'clear'.*

DRESSING FOR DRINK

◆

Red Wine is generally taken in a dinner jacket, for, unless you are a student or a gentleman of the road, you are not drinking red wine without food. The only exception is if drinking wine from an animal hide sack, in which case you are in Spain, fighting in the Civil War and probably wearing a Gieves & Hawkes greatcoat, bullet belt and boots made from horse hide. *Salud!*

LEGENDS OF LIBATION
Winston Churchill

Winston Churchill once refused to eat anything at the royal banquet of Saudi Arabian king Ibn Saud, simply because no alcohol was served. Churchill politely explained that his rule in life was to drink before, during and after each meal.

But Churchill had a much better reception when, in August 1942, he was invited to a banquet in Moscow with Joseph Stalin. The first meeting with Stalin by the British prime minister was known as 'Operation Bracelet'. The banquet did not proceed well at first; Stalin's demands were not to Churchill's liking, and at the eleventh hour he requested a private meeting with the Soviet leader. At one o'clock in the morning Sir Alec Cadogan, under-secretary at the foreign office, entered Stalin's private room and saw the following scene: 'There I found Winston and Stalin, and Molotov who had joined them, sitting with a heavily-laden board between them: food of all kinds crowned by a sucking pig

and innumerable bottles. What Stalin made me drink seemed pretty savage. Winston, who by that time was complaining of a slight headache, seemed wisely to be confining himself to a comparatively innocuous effervescent Caucasian red wine. Everyone seemed to be as merry as a marriage bell.'

Negotiations on an East–West alliance continued till 3 am. On the way back Churchill was in a great mood, as Cadogan describes: 'I think the two great men really made contact and got on terms. Certainly Winston was impressed and I think that feeling was reciprocated ... Anyhow conditions have been established in which messages exchanged between the two will mean twice as much, or more, than they did before.'

Winston Churchill would always start the day with a Johnnie Walker and water, which his daughter called the 'Daddy Cocktail'. He would keep this topped up throughout the day, regarding it more as mouthwash than a drink. His reputation as a heavy drinker was established early in his career: when he was covering the Second Boer War in 1899 as a correspondent for the *Morning Post*, Churchill went to the front with 36 bottles of wine, 18 bottles of Scotch and six bottles of brandy.

Churchill had an enormous capacity for alcohol but was rarely ever seen drunk. He had been taught by his father 'to have the utmost contempt for people who get drunk.' Certainly he could hold his liquor. When he visited the White House, President Roosevelt instructed the staff to adapt to 'Winston Hours.' The President reputedly needed ten hours of sleep a night for three nights, just to recover from a visit from Churchill. However, Churchill did not care for Roosevelt's version of a Dry Martini. His own gin/vermouth ratio was radically different: 'I would like to observe the vermouth from across the room while I drink my martini.' To this day, a 'Churchill Martini' is gin poured over ice, while vermouth is presented in the same room.

Churchill was an enormous fan of champagne. 'A glass lifts the spirits and sharpens the wits – but a bottle produces the opposite effects.' His preferred fizz was Pol Roger. After the liberation of Paris, he attended a lunch at the British Embassy in November 1944, where he and Odette Pol Roger established a friendship that would last for the rest of his life. Every year on Winston's birthday, a case of Pol Roger would be sent to Chartwell. When Churchill died in 1965, Pol Roger placed a black border around its labels, and Pol Roger's prestige champagne Cuvée, released in 1984, was named after Winston Churchill.

CHAPTER 5

FORTIFIED WINE

Masters of the Universe

THE SPARK that detonates and unifies the true character of all fortified wine is the heady level of booze snaking invisibly like a Black Ops fire serpent in every bottle. Fortified wines are not for the faint-hearted and it is said that sipping such drinks regularly will not only 'put hairs on your chest' but also potentially carpet your entire body in a thick pelt of woolly fuzz. And that, by the way, includes the palms of your hands. The most unfortunate case probably ever documented was Margot Lescombes, who, in her infamous Parisian salon party of 1804 sipped a modest glass of what has been reported as 'Sang du Diable', a legendary southern French fortified wine from the extinct L'Enfer grape variety. After a few short moments, Madame Lescombes is said to have immediately transformed into a braying she-ape, with horrified onlookers shaving her as quickly as the hair would sprout. The poor thing expired that night from being cooked in her own hair, such was the power of the insulation, with the hair explosion filling her entire apartment and billowing out on to the street below. Lescombes' Law serves as a reminder that, while fortified wine is capable of igniting a scrumptiously warming sensation of under-floor heating for the soul, you must at all times remember that we are but giddy moths circling a belching inferno that makes Krakatoa seem like the gentle sigh of a mildly disappointed hamster.

THE POWER OF PORT

Britain is the power behind port. We love the stuff and we more or less invented it when, in 1678 we decided (yet again) that we properly hated the French and banned the import of their wine. The Methuen Treaty of 1703 boosted trade between Britain and Portugal and we found their wines to be a bit wimpy, tending to disintegrate during the crossing over the bumpy Bay of Biscay. But a historical technique, reputed to be discovered by a couple of English merchants in the 1670s on a buying trip at the monastery of Lamego, involved boosting the wine by adding brandy. Bingo time! Today, the irony is that, while we Brits were present at port's inception and feel like we own the stuff, it's actually the French who are the largest consumers of this fiery liquid fruit fuel.

The Douro Valley is where port is made and its recipe is simple: crush grapes in 'lagares' (shallow foot treading troughs, today mainly mechanised), stop their fermentation early by adding spirit, which leaves a stack of fruity sweet flavour. Easy. In practice there are a billion factors that make one port

different from another, including the site of the vineyard, yields, soil, grape varieties, age of the vines and so on. The key to the roots of every bottle lies in the unique local grapes that make up the blend, such as Touriga Nacional, Touriga Franca and Tinta Barroca. You also find Tinta Roriz, which is the same as Tempranillo, the headline grape in the Spanish red blends of Rioja (see page 53). Up in the Douro Valley, summers are pretty much as hot and inhospitable as the scenes from Mars in *Total Recall* where Arnold Schwarzenegger's space helmet cracks and his eyes pop out like fried eggs. And the winters can make Narnia look like Mallorca. Not ideal for gently and slowly maturing wine. So, each spring, the new wines are sent down river from the estates (called *quintas*) to take their ease in so-called lodges in Vila Nova de Gaia on the coast, where the 550-litre casks are known in the trade as 'pipes'.

And now, here's the vital intel that every chap should indelibly scrawl on a mental post-it note and leave on the brain door. So strap in and blast off for a heady tasting tour.

THE GALAXY OF PORT

VINTAGE PORT: Ming the Merciless of Port, Ruler of the Galaxy and capable of great ageing if cellared correctly. Harvested from a particularly special year – not every year – these beasts are fulsome, fruity, rich and spicy and really shouldn't be tackled until they are over twenty years of age. They are bottled after two years and do most of their evolution in bottle, and therefore must be stored correctly at an even temperature of 8–10°C out of sunlight. The effect of ageing is to soften and deepen the texture and flavours of this sumptuous, kingly drink that, like Federer versus Nadal, provides a tantalising counterblast of sweetness when paired with salty Stilton. Their union is born of the textural balance and the mimicry of their intensity, while the flavours themselves do sexy fighting on your palate before reaching an entente cordiale when you finally dispatch them to Tummyland.

SINGLE QUINTA VINTAGE PORTS: are the product of a single estate. Great names in port include Taylor's and Warre's, but in our view the apotheosis of port is Quinta do Noval's Nacional – a port so fine, so scented, so supreme and so awesome that we always kneel before the first glass in reverence, and utter the Prayer of Port:

> *Oh grape of Port. You are quite round*
> *A shapely nought, yet deep treasure*
> *Glimmers from your measure. Thanks*
> *For fermenting in tanks*
> *Thou resplendent flavour bomb.*
> *Keep on keepin' on.*

LBV: Late Bottled Vintage Port. This is an affordable yet excellent style of port that should be the mainstay of every chap's drinks cabinet. Not necessarily from a 'declared' year of vintage port but still from a specific year. Worth considering that in non-declared years, grapes that would usually end up in the top class Vintage Port probably make their way into LBV, which makes it a bit of a steal. Cask aged for four to six years, these babies are the Boba Fett of port – always standing by for versatile deployment. Decant and anoint yourself in LBV as often as you dare.

RUBY PORT: does not belong in a chap's digestive tract. Nor do **Reserve Ruby** ports. Though ready to drink, they tend to be sweet and harsh and we feel they detract from the wonder of port's overall pedigree and quality. These are the Cybermen of the Port Galaxy. Not much to tell them apart and generally untrustworthy.

WHITE PORT: Mix it with tonic, ice and a slice of lemon instead of your G&T. The Tweekie of the Port Galaxy (see the 1979 film *Buck Rogers In the 25th Century* starring Gil Gerrard).

TAWNY PORT: is Ridley Scott's *Aliens*. Epic and terrifying. Avoid the cheap stuff simply labelled 'Tawny Port'; this is the alien itself and might gestate inside you before bursting out at dinnertime, frightening off the neighbours and spoiling the soufflé. **Reserve Tawny Ports** can be easy sippers and are generally blended and aged for more than seven years. But the Ellen Ripley, the star of this show, is Tawny with an indication of its age, which is an average of the Tawny Ports blended, not a minimum. They can be 10, 20, 30, even 40 years old and take on the character and intensity of a flaming sultana the size of the sun. Serve chilled with salted

SHERRY

———//———

'There is no year for sherry, 007' croons M with confidence in *Diamonds Are Forever*. And he's got a point – sherry is fractionally blended over many years in a 'solera' system. Yet Bond, with his laser palate, is able to detect the faintest molecules back to the very first year and barrel of this particular bottle, and calls it with cool implausibility: 'I was referring to the original vintage on which the sherry is based sir. 1851. Unmistakable.' It is, in reality, impossible to detect a single year in sherry and that is its very seamless beauty. Drink sherry and you are sipping communal time, the collective efforts of many harvests and many summers, all of which is reflected in its intense wealth of complexity as one of the world's finest drinks. All the stars twinkling across the universe itself are sherry in its true guise. It can be divided into planets, solar systems and galaxies, but sherry is about unity in many. Every bottle is a fortress containing an army of excellence. And you, with admirable insight and taste, should be their Commander in Chief every single night of the year.

THE FOUR CORNERS OF THE SHERRY COMPASS

ALBARIZA: The North Star of sherry. This is the chalky, near-iridescent soil that drains well yet retains moisture and gives finesse to the grapes.

PALOMINO: The eastern dawn where most sherry begins, this grape is behind much of the label, with its low acidity and surprising delicacy.

PEDRO XIMENEZ: The rich setting sun in the west, PX is the sweet white grape, which enriches many styles of sherry and can sometimes be found as a solo act.

FLOR: The indispensable southern root, the yeast of sherry that forms a protective blanket over the liquid in the barrel, lending a discreet nuttiness, and, by being present or absent, it determines the very identity and destiny of every barrel's unique flavour.

Through fractional blending in the **solera** system, which is the compass itself around these four points, the various types of sherry are created with their intensely bold kaleidoscope of character. The solera is the local way of blending across different butts in groups called *criaderas* or nurseries. Older wines are refreshed with younger wines seamlessly through several stages of *criaderas* until the final stage, which is the solera itself. Let's welcome the stars of sherry to the stage like heroes of the music hall, showing their day is far from done as they juggle, conjure, whoop and defy gravity with their golden splendour.

ILLO MANZANILLA: The Ballerina. The lightest and brightest of all sherries. The prima ballerina of our music hall brigade, with breezy poise, power and delicacy. Manzanilla comes from Sanlúcar de Barrameda, a dusty little village on the Costa de La Luz of Andalucía, where the cool maritime influence allows the blanket of flor in every barrel to flourish, sealing freshness into the wine. These are bright tangy fortified wines to chill and sip with green olives in the spirit of party invigoration. Drink them as young and fresh as possible. The bottle, that is, not you. Unless you happen to be young and fresh yourself, in which case this fortified wine is you. And check the bottling date on the bottle for the most recent month you can find.

FINO: The Escapologist. The town of Jerez gives its anglicised name to all sherry, but Fino is the star that ducked under the walls, unshackled its manacles and reached out to a whole new generation of sherry fans the world over. Slightly nuttier and richer than Manzanilla, it remains bright, fresh and, just like Manzanilla, makes great party fuel. The younger and fresher the better, serve it chilled with Iberico ham for one of the simplest and greatest combinations your face will ever feel. Also great with shellfish, olives, Manchego cheese, disco dancing (whatever that is) and cuddles.

AMONTILLADO: The Strong Man! This is a Manzanilla or Fino that breaks through its layer of flor after around seven years, hence the Strong Man. If a drink could wear a unitary and brandish dumbbells, this would be it, as Amontillado tends to be greater in booze than a Fino and more powerful with a nutty savoury richness, thanks to oxidation once the layer of flor has passed away. Avoid the cheap commercial stuff that has been sweetened, the real Strong Man is tangy, rich and a fantastic sherry to serve with hard full-flavoured cheeses such as Parmesan or Cheddar and supreme with slices of Iberico ham or, if you're feeling indescribably sleazy, a packet of pork scratchings. But for Olly, it's a silent solo sip served lightly chilled as he calmly salutes the bottle and murmurs one of his many drinking mottos: 'Always sip better than the best.'

PALO CORTADO: The Invisible Man. Hardly ever found, this enigmatic sherry is similar to a true Amontillado in that it was a sherry destined to be a Fino but whose flor has died away. Tends to be similar to Amontillado but with a richer body, more like a dry Oloroso (see below). If you spot it, buy it and pair it with duck, rabbit or pâté.

OLOROSO: The Conjuror, the sherry with many faces. The meaning of 'Oloroso' is fragrant or smelly, but that really doesn't help much with understanding this powerful sherry, which is always oxidised right from the start of its career. Deeply coloured with big bold flavours, this sherry can be dry, medium or sweet when it is enriched with a splash of sticky Pedro Ximénez (see below) and is known as Cream Sherry. Dry Oloroso is sublime with rich game dishes and even black pudding, whereas Cream Sherry is brilliant with blue cheese or anything with dried fruit that's Christmas-themed, such as a mighty mince pie.

PEDRO XIMENEZ: The Flying Trapeze of sherry – in theory it should be a disaster, but it defies all expectations to deliver the ride of your tiny taste buds' lives. So sweet it should probably be illegal, it's made from sun-dried grapes and is so dark it looks like a melted stick of liquorice has splurged into your glass. Amazing with dark chocolate, it is also outstanding poured over vanilla ice cream – serve a scoop in an espresso cup and drench it with this sweet dark sticky mayhem. If a fig and a date collided in the Realm of Sultanas, this booze tastes like licking the fallout.

THE RING OF FIRE

———— // ————

There are plenty of other fortified wines stretching around the world like a ring of fire. Banyuls, Rivesaltes and Maury are French fortified wines with port-like appeal based on the Grenache grape, with 'rancio' on the label indicating aged styles with a seriously rich flavour, like an espresso made from walnuts. Lighter styles of French fortified wine are made from the white grape Muscat, such as Muscat de Beaumes de Venise and

Muscat de St-Jean de Minervois, which tend to be scented and sweetly fragrant. Further afield, Australia produces Rutherglen Muscat, which is utterly glorious and tastes like liquid Christmas cake, with a discreet echo of explosives in every sip. Such wines are to be taken neat, unlike the fortified power of vermouth.

Ah! To drink, to dream and to raise one's Chalice of Regret to the heavens in defiance of the hangover, which, as we will soon reveal, does not, in fact, need to exist at all.

THE LEGEND OF THE SIX-BOTTLE MEN *In his 1814 reminiscences, Captain Gronow, a contemporary of uber-dandy Beau Brummell, recalled:*

> *'Many men still living must remember the couple of bottles of port at least which accompanied his dinner in those days. There were then four- and even five-bottle men, and the only thing which saved them was drinking very slowly, and out of very small glasses. The late Lords Panmure, Dufferin and Blayney, wonderful to relate, were six-bottle men at this time; and I really think that if the good society of 1815 could appear before their more moderate descendants, in the state they were generally reduced to after dinner, the moderns would pronounce their ancestors fit for nothing but bed.'*

When we try to imagine, today, consuming six bottles of port – even six glasses seems a lot – we realise that men were made of sterner stuff in the Regency period. Arguments were settled by duels, kings consulted dandies on cravat knots (alright, not always manly) and drinking was a test of one's manhood: 'They tell me, Sir John,' said King George III to one of his courtiers, 'that you love a glass of wine'.

'Those who have informed your majesty,' came the reply, 'have done me a great injustice. They should have said a bottle.'

Sir Kingsley Amis, incredulous that anyone in history ever drank more than him, pooh-poohs the whole six-bottle man notion, claiming that port in the early 19th century was more like today's wine in strength. Also, bottles were smaller and more randomly shaped, being hand blown rather than factory produced. Even so, six bottles of red wine? 'If the thought is slow to come, a glass of good wine rewards it.' Drinking was so fashionable that if the Prince Regent turned up to an evening party after an afternoon drinking session, he would be declared unfit for purpose.

VERMOUTH, HERBACIOUS HEAVEN IN A GLASS

———————//———————

'Vermouth is a French or German attempt to say "Wormwood".
Could the idiocy, or bloody foolishness, which comes to afflict the
multi-martini man be the result of the wormwood in the
Vermouth? No, it is the alcohol, you see.'   KINGSLEY AMIS

Sir Kingsley can always be relied upon to cut to the chase when it comes
to drinks around which a certain mythology swirls, like fumes rising
from an Absinthe glass. Vermouth is one of those drinks. Wormwood
historically was a cure for intestinal worms. It is also the Russian for
'Chernobyl'. Other sippage scholars say the word comes from the
German 'wermut', which loosely means 'man with courage or spirit', and
thus the myth deepens and draws us into its mysteries.

Once one enters the world of cocktails, vermouth seems to be everywhere, yet discreetly keeping its own counsel. For many men, the idea of
vermouth is appealing, desirable and, on the surface, easily available, yet
their understanding of it is fragmented, vague and often based on
conflicting experiences. In this sense vermouth occupies a similar place
in a chap's mind as women do.

Vermouth is a fortified aromatised wine infused with herbs and spices
and lurking around 16–20 percent in strength. As we all know, it mixes
well with other drinks and forms, if not the principal base, then an
essential part of many essential cocktails. Alright, so it works very well in
conjunction with other spirits, a bit like a priest, but what can it do on its
own? In the sartorially questionable 1970s, Gustav recalls observing his
parents drinking Martini Rosso on the rocks, and then Leonard Rossiter
backed this up by spilling Cinzano all over Joan Collins, in an
advertisement that has come to symbolise an entire generation of gauche,
be-blazered, aspirational suburban men, whose first-ever foreign holiday
to Malta in 1975 had turned them overnight into a continental
sophisticate. Or at least until the duty-free vermouth ran out.

Vermouth may have belonged to those men then, but today we can
take it back. We can start this by looking at the origins of vermouth. The
Greeks and Romans brewed a herb-infused medicinal drink with
vermouth-like properties, but the man who first created it purely for
pleasure was Antonio Benedetto Carpano of Turin. He began making

vermouth for King Victor Amadeus III, ruler of Piedmont-Sardinia from 1773 to 1796. The Piedmontese began exporting vermouth, with great success. It became so popular in South America that, until the 1950s, in Argentina the 'hour' between six and nine pm was known as 'the Vermouth'. Theatres would advertise 'the vermouth performance' of a play. Olly regularly contacts Gustav with the simple missive saying 'Pub. Vermouth o'clock?'

CONSIDER THE HERBS

'Several times a year a young Italian man-about-town, descending from a family of noble and ancient lineage, parks his Ferrari outside a low stone building, part of a cluster of factory-like structures near Torino. Inside he sheds his cashmere sports jacket and walking stick in exchange for a leather apron and a shovel. There, for an hour or two, behind locked doors and amid bins and boxes of macerated herbs, spices and drugs from far continents, he compounds according to a memorised formula a several-hundred-pound mixture of flavours and aromas which, when added to wine, will carry his family's name and secret around the world in the form of Vermouth.'   *ESQUIRE DRINK BOOK, 1957*

Let's call that man Luciano and let's be honest, his descendant probably isn't doing that today. His poorly paid factotum is, while Luciano II himself strolls along the seafront at Capri with his pink sweater nonchalantly draped over his shoulders. However, today the same herbs are still macerated, and then added to a base of white appetiser wine, which has been given an alcoholic kick from grape brandy. It then takes six months to two years to complete the process of turning wine into vermouth. The herbs, used mainly in their whole form of leaves, roots, flowers, seeds, peel and berries, include:

ANGELICA – fragrant and stimulating

CALAMUS ROOT – formerly used for treating dyspepsia and stomach troubles

CHAMOMILE – scented and bitter, formerly used to cure toothache

JUNIPER – piercing flavour

LEMON BALM – soothing and calming

LUNGWORT – good for lung complaints and coughs

PEPPERMINT, YARROW, WORMWOOD (AT LAST!), VALERIAN AND GENTIAN – good for a sore throat and syphilis

While no vermouth-maker is allowed to make any claims as to its medicinal properties - notably its power to cure intestinal worms - it is quite clear even from the partial list already mentioned that the bottle of vermouth in your drinks cabinet is probably the healthiest potion you possess. Why, with that packet of extra-strong soluble aspirin you keep for hangovers, you are practically a qualified apothecary!

However, even in vermouth's early days, not all its uses were medicinal: Lucullus of Rome (118–57/56 BC) said this: 'Take elecampane, the seeds of flowers, vervain and berries of mistletoe. Beat them, after being well dried in an oven, into a powder and give it to the party you design upon in a glass of wine, and it'll work wonderful effect to your advantage.' So this Roman bounder was making a very early form of vermouth with which to seduce the ladies. What an absolute rotter!

These days, vermouth has spread its wings from its traditional heartland of France and Italy around the world and can be found in more guises than Sherlock Holmes rummaging in his costume box after a spot of naughty smoking. White, pink and red vermouth all belong in a chap's arsenal, with red vermouth as a third of the line-up in the Negroni, along with fine gin and a dose of Campari. In terms of brands, we can happily say we have sampled a great deal. In fact, during their 'Vermouth Off', Olly and Gustav found themselves lost in a whirling dance of such courage and stamina that some six weeks afterwards they were still locked in the deep embrace of their very own dance-step 'The Aromatiser'. So herewith two suggestions beyond the usual suspects of Noilly Prat (white) and Antica Formula (red).

REGAL ROGUE from Australia creates modern vermouth with such intensely splendid flavours that Olly and Gustav are happy to sip them naked over ice. That's the drinks, not the chaps.

BELSAZAR Vermouth from Germany is the kind of brand that happens once in a generation. All of their offerings – dry, red, rosé and white – are worthy of a place in a chap's booze locker. And they should be sipped with carefree abandon.

One final note. Like a splendid peal of laughter echoing around the halls of the gods, vermouth fades fast. Once opened it is prone to oxidation, which means you need to sip it ideally that same day. No hardship, since it tastes so very fine.

DRESSING FOR DRINK

◆

Port, marsala, madeira and sherry should be consumed in a velvet smoking jacket, dress trousers with a single silk stripe down the side (unless you are American, in which case two stripes), black velvet slippers (not monogrammed) and a smoking hat, if you're smoking. If you aren't smoking, what are you doing in a smoking jacket?

CHAPTER 6

THE BRAVADO OF BEER

BEER, like Bond, is divided into two categories: classic and modern. In the same way that Connery and Craig have their differences, so too there are similarities between an old school brown beer in a jug at the pub, or the intensely upbeat vigour of a craft beer served in a tulip-shaped glass. Beer is a global wonder and, as one of the historical leaders in brewing, Britain should be far prouder of its homegrown brews. It is the champagne and champion of our islands and the envy of the world over. In the same way that Englishmen like us might consider pootling down to Château Margaux to take a wistful photo dressed as Withnail in front of the gates, so drinks aficionados flock to Britain to marvel and revel in the feast of ancient breweries dotted liberally around the country, to be photographed before their gates dressed as Oliver Reed. How heartening to see so much respect for the craft of brewing but too often it comes from beer fans abroad. It's time for a bolder approach and for every chap in Britain to stand up and embrace the bravado of beer. Let us doff our caps to the work of our own islands, and then raise it with gratitude to our global partners for taking the beer ball and bouncing it into another dimension.

WHAT THE DEVIL IS BEER?

We know that the Egyptians were sort of brewing around 3000 BC and the flavour of beer as you and we would describe it is broadly derived from malted barley flavoured with hops. The German purity law, or *Reinheitsgebot*, originally declared that only barley, hops and water (with yeast) could be used for making beer, but in 1988 the EU declared it an impingement to free trade and it was withdrawn – but it gives an idea of the beer basics. The reality today is that beer has

---

BEER IS FOR CHAPS *Far from being the province of Rugger Buggers and Lager Louts, beer is now firmly established as diverse, civilised and a great excuse to travel the world from Belgium to Japan, New Zealand to the USA, and sip one's way round the frontiers of flavour. But, of course, every chap will inevitably migrate back to Blighty, finally to perch and roost beside the great honourable slab in a wizened old hostelry, to revel in the very roots of good taste in our admirable islands.*

become insanely creative and brewers can hurl pretty much anything into their brews, from chocolate to pink peppercorns. Brace yourself, chaps, for the new frontier of beer.

THE CONTENTS OF YOUR BEER

Beer is made from four primary ingredients, each endowing it with certain attributes:

HOPS

Hops contribute a huge dose of flavour to beer, ranging from bitter to tropical. You could compare them to the grape varieties of wine, such is their diversity and range. They are grown all over the world, from the USA to Britain, New Zealand, India and beyond. There are four so-called 'noble' hops:

HALLERTAU – light and scented
SAAZ – zing and bite
SPALT – bright bitter spice
TETTNANG – floral aroma

But that's the tip of the iceberg. In the UK you find hops such as Fuggles, which is gently herby for traditional beers, but over in the USA you can find new hops being bred such as Citra, which, as the name suggests is buzzing with fresh exotic citrus flavours. Quite often craft beers are generous enough to list the names of the hops used in them, so a discerning chap, with a small amount of research, can swiftly divine what the beer might taste like.

MALTS

Barley, wheat or rye are steeped in warm water to simulate spring growing conditions, they then sprout and allow the brewer to steal the natural sugars released. The length of time the malt is kilned for has a big impact on the colour of the final beer, from a light Pilsner malt to a deep dark chocolate malt that might be used in a stout. You can even smoke the malt to create a smoked beer, or Rauchbier, and malts can roughly be divided into base (a brew's foundation) and speciality (used sparingly to give character).

WATER

Water is the largest component of any brew, around 95 percent in fact. Historically the geology of the well from which the water was drawn gave character to the brew, from soft water to a water high in mineral salts, such as Burton on Trent, whose waters are so packed with goodies that they give a sulphuric scent known as 'Burton Snatch' – which, by chance, is Olly's pseudonym when he drinks beer alone in Munich. Today any brewery can create their own type of water with their own secret balance of mineral salts, which creates a broad platform from which their brewing identity springs.

YEAST

Many breweries keep their own yeast bank alive on site to maintain consistency from brew to brew. But using different strains of yeast can impart huge character to a particular beer, for example, the banana-tinged character of a German Hefeweisen.

GLASSWARE

The pint glass is standard, the jug is a great comforter, but the truth is the range of flavours and textures in beer is just as sophisticated as those of wine. Glassware has a huge impact on enjoyment of one's brew and it's well worth experimenting with the multitude of shapes on offer, from goblet for Dubbels to bowl for stouts. On the whole, though, a large tulip-shaped stemmed beer glass offers the maximum amount of aroma and flavour. Spiegelau make a good one, and beer connoisseurs should also consider visiting winerackd.uk and enquire about the Beer Anorak DB-Beer Glass.

THE RETURN OF THE JUG *Since 2001, chaps have been nervously watching the hands of barmen and barladies every time they reach for a glass. Yes, it is true: the dimpled pint jar nearly disappeared entirely from our pubs. In 2001, Ravenhead Glass in St Helens – the last UK factory to make dimpled beer glasses – closed forever. What were we to do? Could a gentleman really drink beer from a straight glass, and regard his companions over the top of it with anything except deep everlasting shame and humiliation? He might call it a pint pot. He may simply call it a jug. But during the dark days of the 1970s and 80s, glasses in pubs grew taller and lost their dimples and handles, like some grotesque form of enforced evolution by a race of robot warriors. Once Ravenhead Glass closed, it looked as though chaps would be forced to join the lager-swilling lads with their imbecilic straight glasses, which many bar staff secretly preferred as they are easier to wash and stack. But then, our saviour arrived in the unlikely form of hipster bars in trendy parts of London. The craft and micro-brewery vogue brought with it a wistful nostalgia for the dimpled pint glass. A Turkish supplier was found and soon all the bearded chaps in their lumberjack shirts were standing at the bars of old pubs, now run by micro-breweries, swilling craft ales from jugs. Our view is that it doesn't really matter why they came back, it is simply joyous that we have a choice as to what shaped glass to quaff our beloved ale from.*

THE ENGLISH PUB

The gentle murmur of voices. The clink of glasses. The slosh of dark ale filling a tankard. The pop of a crisp packet being opened. A round of laughter. The crackle as a log is popped on the fire. An old man in a flat cap bustling in, shutting the door on the gusts outside. 'Half of mild and bitter, if you please.'

Where are we, in a dream? An Ealing Comedy? Paradise itself? No, gentlemen, we are in the 21st century and thanking the Lord for the preservation of the English pub. An institution that has remained unchanged, in many of its better exponents, since medieval times. And even the ones that have evolved, by removing the horse brasses and painting the walls grey, have still maintained some vital essence of the original inns of these fair isles, which distinguishes them from all the other drinking holes of the world.

The Spanish have their *bodegas*, the French their *bar-tabacs*, the Germans their *bierkellers*, the Americans their bars, all of which are fine and dandy for chaps on their hols seeking a refreshing local tipple, but there is nothing quite like entering an English pub on a cold winter's night. Even on a sunny afternoon, it is always winter in a pub. The light from outside might try to penetrate the gloom and remind you that there is something else to do, but seriously, is there?

What activity on God's Green Earth could be more civilised, more important and more invigorating than sitting (we'll come to standing up in pubs later) at a slightly sticky table with several beer mats propping up one of the legs, and discussing practically anything with one's favourite chums? There is something about an English pub that encourages fine conversation as soon as one enters – although do read 'Types of Drunk' for the caveats (see page 152). Pubs are like the Symposia of Ancient Greece; one pulls an imaginary toga over one's head upon entry and sharpens up one's wit and intelligence for the debate ahead. This could be about whether Britain was right to reject the European Exchange Rate Mechanism or whether five pence coins are prettier than half pennies.

Pubs have a place in every stage of our lives. At the beginning of a relationship they provide a neutral yet cosy venue for quiet discussions that may lead to love. Though often small, pubs, even those without music, somehow encourage privacy among the customers, if that is what they require. One may visit the same pub a week after one's first date and be absorbed by a huge, beery, happy crowd that shuns privacy in favour of bonhomie and unity. When you stand among such folk at the bar of your local; young, old, male, female, human, canine, equine (in some country pubs) you are truly part of the community and there is no need to worry about anything at all, apart from whose round it is. Everyone, at least once in their lives, should enter their local pub and offer to buy every single punter a drink. When you choose to do this is up to you: in Gustav's case it was when his tailor had finally agreed to put turned-back cuffs on his jacket; in Olly's it was when his pet python Arabella gave birth to triplets, giving rise to the cheery toast of 'Snake Surprise!'

TYPES OF BEER AND FOOD PAIRINGS

This is by no means an exhaustive list but the six worldwide headliners every chap needs to order with confidence are nestling within these lines. Rather like the instruments of an orchestra, so different beers have their own unique character, whether as light and bright as a piccolo or deep and resonant as a trombone. 'Timothy Trombone' is, incidentally, Gustav's nomenclature when sipping beer alone in the souks of Cairo.

PILSNER: THE VIOLIN. Bright and zesty as the sound of a fiddle on a springtime breeze, this pale lager was born in Bohemian *Plzeň* or Pilsen, which today is part of the Czech Republic. Until the 1800s, most beers were 'top-fermented', giving a richer brew, but fermenting the yeast on the bottom and storing in cool caves (lagers) gave rise to this brighter upbeat apéritif-friendly style. It's also the balls with fish and chips.

HEFEWEISEN: THE CLARINET. Originally from southern Germany, this wheat beer, just like the sound of a clarinet, is gently fruity – think bananas and cloves. A must for a chap's midweek sharpener that works a treat with Thai food.

FRUIT BEER: THE CORNET. Jazz attack! Behold these beauties of Belgium and beyond! A whole load of styles here from the whole fruity spectrum, look out for Kriek (cherry) to Framboise (raspberry). Just like the cornet, they can have a thrilling edge of sharpness and, unlike the cornet, generally have brisk bubbles thanks to carbonation. A fruity Kriek beer can be stunning paired with Bakewell tart. And when you raise your glass, you must in no way behave ironically. Roger Moore eyebrow curls are strictly forbidden at this juncture.

IPA: THE FRENCH HORN. India Pale Ale tends to be as resonant as a French horn as well as enthrallingly bitter, thanks to a turbo injection of hops but also with a fruity thunder rolling in the background. These beers are full flavoured and can change the course of your day with their instant power-thrust — also an excellent restorative after an impertinent encounter, such as a dachshund passionately rutting at your ankle. Can work brilliantly with a dirty burger or with fragrant spicy dishes such as Vietnamese.

BITTER: THE CELLO. Every chap's favourite. Classic British brown beer with a malty belly that's as rich as the sound of a cello drifting from the open window of an extremely clever yet mildly lonesome hero in an Edwardian detective story set in Cambridge. Bitter is, of course, the ultimate Ploughman's companion or the perfect backdrop to the best conversation of your life. Chaps really ought to be swimming in this stuff on a regular basis — and we do not mean 'flippers and frogman', we mean buttock-winkingly nude.

STOUT: THE DOUBLE BASS. Dark, bouncing, rich and creamy, this beer makes an amazing partner to a 3pm chocolate brownie. A little of this deep rumbling double bass of a beer goes an awfully long way. Deploy at teatime or as a game-changer when a rogue aunt comes into play. She will love it and you will love her more.

TYPES OF PUB

In the old days, pubs were all more or less the same: a floor full of sawdust, a room full of men and beer pulled straight from the barrel. The only decoration was the sign on the wall that read: DRUNKARDS WILL BE HANGED and NO URINATING ON THE FLOOR. These days, there are all manner and variety of hostelries, from rough-house boozer to sophisticate's retreat. Here is a handy list of the types of pub you will encounter on these isles and what to expect therein:

YOU DON'T HAVE TO BE LOCAL TO DRINK HERE (BUT YOU DO)

Décor: Threadbare carpet in shades of red, horse brasses, photos of the pub 100 years ago (looking exactly the same as today). Clientele: males, 50+ (and that includes their dogs). Lavatories: pungent, abandoned. The menu: principally real ales, a few perfunctory bottles of lager, good selection of single malt. Catchphrase: 'Fred's in late tonight.' (at 5pm).

THE CITIZEN'S ADVICE BUREAU

Décor: grey walls, large photographs of pebbles. Clientele: boring people in their late 30s. Lavatories: pointlessly wallpapered. The menu: craft ales, lots of Czech lager, tons and tons of red wine at eye-watering prices and a vast range of glass sizes. Catchphrase: 'A small-to-semi-medium Shiraz please, and some of those overpriced macadamia nuts.'

THE WILD WEST SALOON

Décor: Carpet decorated with wet patches, broken chairs, passport photos of youths barred for life. Lavatories: dangerous. The menu: Lager, lager lager. Catchphrase: 'Wot you lookin' at, mate?' (to the landlord as he pulls pint).

LADIES' NIGHT

Décor: bare, polished floorboards, framed reproduction wartime posters. Lavatories: lovely. The Menu: white wine, sparkling wine, rosé wine, weak beer. Catchphrase: 'Is she really going out with him?'

ALE V. BEER

Until around 1400, the ingredients of ale consisted of malted barley, water and yeast, with the occasional herb such as rosemary thrown in for good measure. In the 15th century hops were added, inspired by the beers brought over from Flanders and Holland. These were more bitter and longer-lasting, thanks to the hops, and they came to be known as beer, while the old variety stuck with the name of ale. Henry VIII, never one to miss out on more boozing, employed two brewers to supply Hampton Court Palace, one bringing ale and the other beer. More than 13,000 pints were consumed each day, and it wasn't just the chaps, either. Ladies-in-waiting were allowed a gallon of beer just for breakfast. Queen Elizabeth I, we are told, rather liked a nice pint too. When travelling around England she would send someone ahead to sample the local ale. If word came back that it wasn't up to scratch, a few barrels of the good stuff would be dispatched from London. She also complained when brewers stopped making what she called 'single' beer and made instead 'a kynde of very strong bere calling the same doble-doble bere, which they do commonly utter and sell at a very grate and excessive pryce.' She should have tried entering a gastro pub in the Home Counties today and trying to get change out of a fiver for a pint of craft ale. Doble-doble beer indeed.

DRESSING FOR DRINK

❖

Being something of a working drink, the work being stimulating conversation with chums, you may relax your dress somewhat in order to consume ale. Your jacket – tweed of course, unless you are in Town – may be draped over the back of your chair, displaying your moleskin waistcoat and your heavy cotton shirt, which you have twinned with a tartan tie. Your trousers are either corduroy or moleskin and your feet are not clad in anything more sinister than a stout pair of brown brogues. Your brown fedora is on the top of your head, because you are the eccentric type who plays with sartorial rules purely because you have such a deep understanding of them that you can.

LEGENDS OF LIBATION
Oliver Reed

Oliver Reed's final bar tab is said to have amounted to an impressive £590.22, in a bar in Malta during the filming of Ridley Scott's Roman epic *Gladiator*. In one evening, Ollie had apparently consumed eight bottles of German beer, three bottles of Captain Morgan's rum and several double Famous Grouse whiskies, supposedly buying rounds for everyone else. The legend continues that he added one more whisky to the tab, but before he could pay, he had collapsed on the floor with a heart attack. One hour later he was stone dead.

The actor David Hemmings claimed that Reed could drink 20 pints of lager with a gin or crème de menthe chaser and still run a mile for a wager. Reed was once reported to have drunk 124 pints of beer in 24 hours, before doing a horizontal handstand on the bar. A regular drinking buddy of Alex Higgins, Reed would apparently spike the dipsomaniac snooker player's whisky with Chanel perfume, to which Higgins is said to have retaliated by squirting washing-up liquid in Reed's crème de menthe.

'I do not live in the world of sobriety,' said Ollie, pretty accurately. He usually started off well, striking the pose of an old-fashioned English gentleman at the beginning of a mammoth drinking session, but by the end resembling more of a Neanderthal beast, barely able to remain on two feet and incapable of speech. That's when he resorted to fighting, a language he spoke fluently. Even when completely bladdered, his eagle eyes kept tabs on all his drinking companions. Should any of them dare to yawn or refuse a drink, they might find themselves thrown down a flight of stairs. 'My only regret,' he once confessed, 'is that I didn't drink every pub dry and sleep with every woman on the planet.'

One night, a number of naked men had been spotted running through a field in

Oakwoodhill, Surrey. When police arrived on the scene, the naturists turned out to be a local rugby team who had been drinking with Ollie, and he had encouraged them all to strip off and tear through the fields around his house. However, Reed was always quick to scotch rumours about his drinking that he felt he hadn't earned. At a controversial stag weekend before his marriage to Josephine Burge, Reed was reported to have drunk 104 pints of ale. 'The event that was reported,' he was quick to correct, 'Actually took place during an arm-wrestling competition in Guernsey about 15 years ago.'

Sometimes Ollie acted, too. Always the consummate professional, he would often swear off the drink when playing a film role, but there were always exceptions: he allegedly needed a bottle of vodka to steady his nerves before the nude wrestling scene in *Women in Love*. When another role required him to lose weight, he is said to have conscientiously put himself on a vodka-only diet for several weeks.

Though regarded as a fine film actor, Reed became better known during his later career for his drunken appearances on television chat shows. During his first appearance on *The Tonight Show*, Shelley Winters poured a glass – or some say a jug – of whisky over Reed's head when he made some misogynistic comments. Reed later stated, 'My row with Shelley Winters was caused by her abominable lack of manners.'

Reed's carousing really came into its own once he bought an enormous mansion in Surrey called Broome Hall. Guests staying for the weekend could never claim that their stay was dull or predictable, or indeed sane.

Party games included playing ice hockey on a kitchen floor slippery with smashed eggs, dancing on the antique dining table, having carved one's name into it with a knife, and, most fun of all, knocking other guests across a nearby stream with a single punch. Friends of Ollie's clad in monk's habits would jump out of cupboards on unsuspecting guests while they dressed for dinner. Once all the guests were finally asleep, Reed is said to have prowled the corridors in the early hours, shooting his own furniture with a shotgun to help him relax.

But Reed was not without his generous side and was always an excellent host. Befriending a fellow drinker at his local, the Cricketer's Arms, Reed, so the story goes, offered to put him up when it was quite clear the man was far too drunk to drive home. When the stranger showed the slightest sign of refusal, Ollie wrestled him to the ground and knelt on the man's neck until he finally said yes.

One guest who gladly accepted Ollie's invitation to stay at Broome Hall was Keith Moon. When they were both cast in *Tommy* in 1975 Moon was so excited about working with Ollie that he took a helicopter to Broome Hall to introduce himself, forgetting to inform Ollie. The helicopter nearly crashed and some horses bolted while Reed was in the bath. Enraged at the commotion, he ran out wearing only a towel, brandishing a broadsword. He and Moon fought for over an hour, ending up on the roof. It was love at first fight. 'We just fell for each other directly,' said Ollie. 'I was taking life a little bit too seriously. Keith showed me the way to insanity.'

CHAPTER 7

CIDER IS WONDERFUL

THE APPLE. So tempting that it's the cause of mankind's moral downfall in the Garden of Eden. But ferment it into a boozy liquid version of itself and it becomes irresistible in the extreme and, along with anticipated turpitude, spiritual exuberance is virtually guaranteed. Sir Kingsley Amis remains curiously silent, in his many volumes on booze, on the subject of cider. Which just goes to show that this mystical, bucolic, sometimes fizzy/sometimes cloudy pagan brew has only recently begun to grace the glass of the gentleman.

'Twas not long ago that cider was erroneously considered one of those drinks whose sole purpose was to bring about drunkenness, as quickly and as cheaply as possible. In some bohemian quarters it was not much further up the Tree of Pleasure than Thunderbird wine or Carlsberg Special Brew, and was often to be found at the ersatz bodega, fashioned from old barrels under a freezing bridge in a city of ill repute, frequented by gentlemen of the road.

However, the apples have ripened for cider and the orchard is bountiful. Hitherto secret potions brewed by farmers in remote Somerset apple farms have gradually filtered into the high street, and one may now purchase a bewildering quantity of brands and different styles of cider that are not named Strongbow or Woodpecker (delicious as those basic forms of cider are – especially

when one is youthful and bonkers in almost equal measure).

Curiously, cider began its journey into our tankards as an early form of money. Farm labourers were paid part of their wages in cider, with the earliest record of this taking place in Norfolk in 1204. This tradition continued, with mixed results – the farms offering the best cider would attract the less problematic workers – until as late as 1887, when a law was passed in Britain prohibiting the payment of workers in cider.

The ease and splendour with which apples may be grown in Britain, from Hereford to Kent and Somerset to Sussex, ensured that cider stuck around as the favoured beverage of the rural classes and, thanks to the Normans, always on the lookout to fiddle about with our blessed nation and change things, many new apple varieties were introduced. At one time there were 365 varieties of cider apple in Britain – that's one different apple for each day of the year! (Except leap years.)

The Bishop of Bath was the first man of the cloth to introduce monks to the joys of cider, and he bought the first commercial cider presses for his monastery in 1230. Monks, as we know, are very good at making alcohol (the naughty buggers) and often come up with the most refined method of production. By the 18th century, cider was being enjoyed by all classes of society, though

possibly not for breakfast by the upper classes. Compared to stronger booze such as port and brandy, cider was seen as 'health-giving', a cure for gentlemanly ailments like gout and scurvy, and a source of goodness for the digestion and the prevention of 'gravel-stone' in the kidneys. None of this was true, of course, but everybody had a modicum of fun and no harm was done.

It was only in the 20th century that a subtle battle began to take place between cider and beer as the drink of choice for the masses. Sometimes this battle took place in one's very glass, in the form of Snakebite. Ask for a pint of this venomous concoction in some pubs and you will be given short shrift. (Curiously, order fifteen large brandies successively and you will be happily served, with probably worse results on your health and on the local masonry.)

Ultimately, beer won this battle – but not the war. Cider has been creeping back into our nation's hostelries in crisper and more refined varieties, and there are now some brands of cider around that if you saw a hobo drinking one of them, you'd be forgiven for suspecting he was an eccentric millionaire in some kind of disguise.

The old method of making cider was to blend various apple types into one brew, but recent trends have been to use a single variety of apple to produce a more elegant cider.

Beware too what some experts term 'false cider': beardy CAMRA types maintain that true cider must be made from 100 percent apples and nothing else. Some of the cheaper brands mix sugar and chemicals in with the apples, which is shocking but certainly have a market.

Ciders come in all sorts of shapes and sizes. From sparkling Breton in France to our British dry medium and sweet farmhouse scrumpy, which is generally still, and even Ice Cider, the perfect accompaniment to an apple tart - or indeed which can be viewed as the very essence of apple tart in a glass. Olly's two favourite places in the world for cider are the English Cider Centre at Middle Farm near Lewes in East Sussex, with a wealth of barrels that can be freely sampled in small jots before pouring your final choices into takeaway plastic containers. But for the greatest experience of sipping cider, the stuff that Charlie makes at the Square & Compass in Dorset's Worth Matravers is miraculous, and the location offers the perfect hilly coastal view to meditate on the moment. Be warned, any more than three pints of this stuff and you may need to lie down and listen to George Harrison's 'My Sweet Lord' a few times to reset your sense of propriety and gravity. At least that's what Olly found on his 40th birthday sipping session at the Square & Compass.

For bottles that you might actually spot in your local outlets, **Cornish Orchards** make a few choice bottles. **Dunkertons** is a name to repeat under your breath. **Thatchers** have some calibre. **Aspall's** Premier Cru and Organic do the job for us. But nothing can beat licking the local stuff and we buy ours from Middle Farm, which also happens to be home to the National Cider & Perry Collection.

PERRY COMO VA

We've all heard of perry and assumed it is just cider made with pears, but is it as simple as that? Like cider, the perry-making process was introduced just after the Norman Conquest, so it would be churlish not to give the French some credit for it. They rather conveniently found that pears seemed to survive in areas where apples did not, particularly in Worcestershire, Gloucestershire, Herefordshire and parts of Wales. This proved very useful to soldiers in the English Civil War billeted in those counties; for revolution, however short-lived its results, is thirsty work. At this stage, English perry was a very dry concoction served straight from the vat, whereas the French version was fizzier, sweeter and served in the bottle.

The labour-intensive farming of perry pears caused the drink to go into a slow decline during the 20th century. It took years to cultivate an orchard of suitable pears and ladies on hen nights simply couldn't wait that long. Perry experienced a revival of sorts in the 1970s, in the form of Babycham, a mass-produced perry aimed at the lower end of the market, made in Somerset by the Showering Company. Served in miniature champagne-style bottles, it was about as far from champagne as one could get without travelling to the Moon on an alcohol-free spaceship.

CALVADOS, FLAMING HEART OF NORMANDY

Calvados occupies a curious place in a chap's drinks cabinet, straddling as it does the glaringly opposed worlds of rustic peasants swigging scrumpy in fields and sophisticated colonels sinking so deeply into wing-backed leather armchairs that search parties have to be sent in for them.

Calvados, a cider spirit, has many similarities to brandy, the first of these being that it is French, although apple brandy is now made elsewhere including the fair shores of Britain. The word itself was in common usage long before the French Revolution, it being much quicker to say 'A flagon of calvados, my good man,' than 'a flagon of eau de vie de cidre, mon brave.' Once the Revolution had divvied up the nation into 83 convenient departments to be lorded over by the new order of non-bluebloods, calvados was one of them, which was convenient as the department already had its own alcoholic beverage and therefore status. The name originally suggested for the region was 'Orne Inférieure', which again one has to admit is not quite as catchy as Calvados: 'We simply must visit Orne Inférieure for a glass of eau de vie de cidre' would not have done much for tourism in the area.

The production of calvados across its 1550 parishes is today strictly controlled in the same way as the production of wine, cognac and champagne. There are three distinct calvados appellations – Calvados, Calvados Pays d'Auge and Calvados Domfrontais.

Plain old **Calvados** can be made from apples or pears (177 varieties are permitted) or a blend of the two and it is distilled in an alembic under continuous distillation. It must be aged in barrel for a minimum of two years and be at least 40 percent.

Calvados Pays d'Auge can only be made in 290 of the 1550 parishes and, like all Calvados, can be made from both apples and pears, but not all versions are.

Calvados Domfrontais is the chap's choice. The rules require that at least 30 percent of pears are added to the distillation. The barrel-ageing process takes a minimum of three years and you can expect a distinctive peardrop aroma from these bottles.

Calvados blending is one of those careers that the really smart kid from your school (if you went to school in upper Normandy) ended up in. A Calvados blender performs a form of alchemy that requires great subtlety and the ability to choose from hundreds of variables such as age, crop and *terroir* to produce the perfect blend. There are no single malts in calvados and the finished product strikes a wonderful balance between woodiness and fruitiness, the flavour of raw apples gradually fading into the flavour of cooked apples and even (it's glorious, honest) rotten apples. A particularly good calvados can be labelled as being up to 25 years old but that only describes the youngest vintage in the bottle, which could contain brandies up to 50 years old, though no younger than 25 years old. The four categories of Calvados are:

Fine, Trois étoiles, Trois pommes or VS (Very Special). Any of these must have been aged in wood for at least two years.

Vieux or Réserve must have been aged for at least three years.

VO (Very Old), Vieille Réserve and VSOP (Very Special Old Pale) must have been aged for at least four years.

Hors d'Age, XO, Très Vieille Réserve, Très Vieux, Extra and Napoléon: these are the big boys (we know that because IL Duce gets a namecheck only at this stage) and require at least six years ageing in wood.

Chaps will want to know their calvados categories because the year stated on the label only guarantees that the fruit was harvested in that year, rather than guaranteeing any particular length of ageing.

WASSAILING *From the old Norse 'Ves Heil', wassailing is an expression that wishes health and also refers to the mulled cider sipped on Twelfth Night during this ritual that wishes for a good harvest. The idea is to wake up the orchard and run off any wicked sprites that may be lingering and inevitably drink a few cups. A wassail king or queen is then hoisted up to place toast soaked in wassail, as a gift to the tree spirits. We love doing it and in fact don't restrict our wassailing to one night. Every night is wassailing night at Chap HQ. Join us.*

DRESSING FOR DRINK

◆

Cider should only ever be drunk within earshot of braying livestock. Wellington boots with baggy corduroy trousers tucked into them form the lower half of the ensemble. The shirt is of course Tattersall and made of brushed cotton; the waistcoat is dun-coloured or brown and does *not* contain a fob watch. The jacket is thornproof tweed, the heaviest you can find, and is allowed to have a few tears and patches here and there. There is a pocket square (there is *always* a pocket square) but it can look as though it has been used to wipe the sweat off a horse recently. The hat, tilted quite far back on the head, is a battered trilby or flat tweed cap – not the eight-sectioned baker-boy variety.

GIN & FIRE

'Liquid Madness sold at tenpence the quarter.' Thus did Thomas Carlyle, admittedly not the world's greatest party animal, describe gin in 1839. Back then, gin was still waiting for its launch into the High Life, and was the tipple of choice for the lower orders of London for at least a century. Gin palaces, glamorous as they sound, were disgusting dives in seedy quarters of the capital where the bottom end of society would spend the evening quaffing crude early forms of Old Tom gin, before sloping off to some hovel or simply bedding down on the floor of the tavern. Some inns had a piece of rope strung before the bar, where patrons could topple into slumber and await their hangovers to grab them at dawn. Others took advantage of the tavern's generous offer: 'Drunk for a penny, dead drunk for tuppence, clean straw for nothing.' Some of these once dreadful establishments survive to this day, though spruced up a bit and no longer offering free straw. The Princess Louise on High Holborn in central London is one, still with the original decorated glass panels and dark wooden balustrades. The gins they serve there now, as we will discover later, are vast improvements on Old Tom.

The origins of the production of gin go back even further than the days when you could spend the night on the floor of the Princess Louise. Gin was invented by a Dutchman named Franciscus de la Boe, also known as Dr Sylvius, who was experimenting with cures for kidney complaints by infusing raw alcohol with juniper, known for its therapeutic properties. He named it *genièvre*, French for juniper, and it proved an instant success – not surprising since anything with a flavour would have been an improvement on the raw alcohol generally consumed in those days. Gin is quite unique, compared to all other spirits, in that the principal flavour, which comes from juniper berries, alongside other botanicals such as coriander and angelica root, as well as a few 'secret' ingredients, depending on the manufacturer, are all fused with a spirit that has already been distilled – basically a vodka. This is unlike the flavours of whisky, brandy, rum and the like, all of which are informed by the base grain, grapes or sugar cane from which they are distilled and created.

Once gin hit Britain's thirsty shores, brought from Holland by soldiers as duty-free gifts for their families, it immediately tickled the palates of the poor and didn't leave that stratum of society for 200 years. One of the causes of its appeal was the introduction of new taxes by William of Orange on the import of French cognac. For some reason he excluded grain-based spirits such as gin (it is worth noting he was born in The Hague and presumably had strong Dutch sympathies) which resulted in a cascade, flood and tidal surge of gin pouring into Britain. By the late 17th century, anyone wishing to set up a gin distillery could do so simply by posting a notice to the public ten days before going into production. This led to the dark days of gin, when any old rubbish, including oil of vitriol and turpentine, was hurled into the stills instead of quality spirit and expensive juniper berries. Such was the addiction of the masses to any and every form of gin that attempts by the authorities to curb production were met with rioting in the streets. It was not until the Tippling Act of 1751 that quality control began to ensure that licensed victuallers provided their customers with gin that might not kill them immediately.

The Dutch, meanwhile, continued to enjoy and distil gin, a row of distilleries sprouting up, and remaining today, along the banks of the Maas River at Schiedam. The tradition began in the 17th century, and also remains to this day, of the *borrel* – partaking in a glass or two of gin. The gin is served at long communal tables and, in the early days of the Dutch Empire, the *borrel* was observed by Dutch plantation supervisors as early as 9.30 am, having been on the job since dawn because of the heat of Java, Sumatra and other islands of the East Indies. Their country clubs would have a special *borrel* table, large and round with a hole in the middle. A small native boy resided in this hole; when the gentlemen required a top-up, they would rap their knuckles on the table and up he would pop with a bottle of gin.

Anyway, back to London please, and never mind what Dutch milords got up to. London Gin, a blend with a unique sense of origin thanks to its fresh bright style, came about in part due to the wonderful natural springs the

SIR ROGER MOORE'S GIN MARTINI *Swoosh a jug with Noilly Prat vermouth and discard. Fill with top-notch gin, pour into cocktail glasses and put into the freezer. Serve frosty with a twist of lemon.*

city boasts, principally at Clerkenwell and Goswell. Not so important today, but back then the purity of the water was a major factor on the quality of the gin, which gradually improved over time, eventually coming to the attention of the upper classes, and particularly the *bon ton* of the Regency himself, always on the lookout for new ways to get utterly plastered. Lord Byron once declared, 'Gin and water is the source of all my inspiration.' But then Gordon (no relation to the gin) was always trying to be outrageous and may have been exaggerating. Incidentally, Kingsley Amis, another boozy *bon vivant*, writing 150 years later, was a huge advocate of gin and water: 'Gin and water is an all-round improvement on gin and tonic: cheaper, less fattening and less filling as well as not being sweet or gassy. Gin is a real and interesting drink, carefully prepared with those botanicals and all, and it deserves to be sampled with its flavour unimpaired.'

Kingsley also makes the point that gin entered the cocktail cabinets of colonial gentlemen residing in hot countries like India when they took quinine to ward off malaria. When quinine was refined into tonic water, someone noticed that the stuff went down a little easier if you chucked some gin into it. The chef Clarissa Dickson Wright lived in India for a spell, and she wondered why she remained immune to the malaria that was knocking down all her ex-pat cohorts, until a doctor pointed out that the vast quantities of gin and tonic she was consuming were acting as an inoculation.

HOW GIN IS MADE

Gin is as wide and wild as the cast of a Dickens novel in that it can be wrought from pretty much any neutral spirit made from a vast range of base agricultural products – sugar beet, grain, apples, molasses and more. The fire in gin comes from the pure spirit, the hidden spark that ignites the fireworks of flavour bestowed by botanicals, the most important of which is juniper. Other aromatic botanicals vary from gin to gin but commonly include angelica, cardamom, coriander, citrus peel and more, either macerated in the neutral spirit before a further distillation or suspended during a further distillation to be infused into the vapour. What we predominantly enjoy in the Greatest of Britains is called London Dry, a bright and zesty style of gin that deploys a superior system of distillation, unlike cold compound gins (which are cheap and best avoided) that rely on flavouring essences instead of raw ingredients.

In recent years, there has been an explosion of new innovative distilleries crafting gin across our shores with a whole host of bonkers botanicals from Africa's baobab fruit as in Whitley Neill to Arbequina olives around the Mediterranean found in Gin Mare. Among the finest in our opinion are:

WARNER EDWARDS HARRINGTON DRY GIN Created by lifelong buddies Tom Warner and Sion Edwards in Harrington, Northamptonshire. With a fragrant dose of cardamom, this was the gin that resulted in the commencement of formal dancing at Olly's 40th birthday celebrations. It is more or less irresistible: an all-round top-notch gin.

SACRED GIN This London Dry Gin is a double gold medal winner forged in a craft distillery hiding in Highgate that began its life in a Wendy house. Microdistiller Ian Hart is a magician of reduced pressure distillation – under a vacuum – which gives his unique gin extraordinary purity and freshness. The distillery takes its names from one of the botanicals in the gin, *Boswellia sacra*, also known as frankincense. We love it served neat from the freezer.

GIN MARE From the shores of Barcelona comes this outrageously delicious Mediterranean gin enriched with savoury finesse from curious botanicals such as basil, thyme, rosemary and Arbequina olives. Served with the exceptional Fever-Tree tonic, we reckon this gin turns a moment into a meditation on the sheer splendour of fine flavour.

XORIGUER From Mahon, the capital of Menorca, this gin is fabulous value and is also, alongside Plymouth, one of the few gins of the world to have a geographical indication – Gin de Menorca. Kicking off with the British occupation in the 18th century, it's made in wood-fired pot stills from distilled wine and spends some time in American oak before bottling. The locals take it as a 'Pomada' in a tall glass packed with ice topped up with real lemonade and a slice of lemon which tends to unleash the hidden fiesta inside us all.

WILLIAMS CHASE ELEGANT GIN Clever kit that deploys apples to create a very fine base spirit on a Herefordshire farm in a still called 'Ginny' which Olly has in fact met. One part Martini to two parts Williams Chase Elegant Gin shaken over ice served in a cold martini glass with a slice of apple is, as Ollie Reed might have said 'marvellous as the thunder of happiness'.

FURTHER GINS OF NOTE These include Sipsmith, Portobello Road, and No. 3 London Dry Gin. Among the big names, don't fear the Beefeater – he will serve every chap sufficiently well in times where choice is as limiting as a posing pouch on a wintery stroll.

Given gin's sensitive balance of botanicals, it is peculiar that it has ended up as one of the most popular bases for cocktails, as well as smothered in tonic, ice and lemon. One explanation for this takes us over to the Americas, where Prohibition brought about the illegal distillation of various spirits in the bathtub, the easiest of which was gin. College boys at Princeton and Harvard would fill a bath with pure alcohol and add a few drops of flavouring bought at a drugstore, stir it a bit and then shove it in cocktails. So gin entered the Ivy League circuit, along with Oxford bags and sharp blazers, in the form of Dry Martinis, Tom Collinses and Gin Fizzes. With today's fine range of gins crafted and wrought from an ever-more inventive catalogue of botanicals, it seems astonishing to mix them with the same old uniform big name of mixers. Quality tonic including those made by Fever-Tree remain your best option for a quality mixer worthy of the finest gin.

GIN RICKEY *A tale still whispered in America that dates from 1915 is of a mysterious man named 'Colonel' Jim Rickey, who usually lurked around the Waldorf Bar in New York. Described as a gentleman of grace and flowing charm, with a luxuriant grey moustache and a black slouch hat, he was something of a connoisseur of drinks and wherever he appeared bartenders would quake in their boots. Once at a New York bar called the Shoemaker he was handed a drink that was currently 'in production' by the staff, consisting of the juice and rind of one lime, a lump of ice, a slug of gin and a charge of water. The Colonel took a sip, flung it down his throat and asked for another. The owner of the bar immediately named it the Gin Rickey and the Colonel himself, spotting an opportunity, entered the business of importing limes.*

THE NAVY LARK *With the invention of the continuous still in the mid-18th century, the more delicately flavoured style of gin came to be known as London Dry, because most distillers were based in London. At the same time the ports of Liverpool, Bristol and Plymouth created their own versions, but only Plymouth Gin survives. For almost two centuries, Her Majesty's Naval Fleet was sustained by Plymouth Gin, and no ship left port without a bottle of Navy Strength 100 proof (57 percent ABV. ABV stands for alcohol by volume in the UK and commonly worldwide but look out for alcohol proof in the USA which is a different way of measuring and doubles the ABV. So a 30 percent ABV in the UK would be 60 percent proof in the USA.) 'Navy Strength' refers to the strength at which a spirit could be spilt on gunpowder and would still ignite. It was a tradition in the Royal Navy that all newly commissioned vessels received a 'Plymouth Gin Commissioning Kit', a wooden box containing two bottles of Navy Strength Plymouth Gin and glassware. Along with the official rum ration – there was clearly no shortage of supplies for high jinks in the Wardroom.*

The original distillery still exists and is one of the oldest buildings in Plymouth, dating back to the early 1400s, as well as England's oldest working distillery, still true to the original recipe created in 1793. Originally a Black Friars monastery, the dissolution of the monasteries in 1536 turned it into a debtor's prison. It became a billet for Huguenot refugees fleeing France, and was the building from which the Pilgrim Fathers made the short walk down to the harbour to set sail on the **Mayflower** *in 1620 to found a New World. The ship forms Plymouth Gin's trademark label today.*

Plymouth Gin is one of the few gins to have an 'appellation controlée' and it can only be made within the walls of the city of Plymouth. It became so popular in the cocktail era of the 1920s that as many as 23 recipes in the **Savoy Book of Cocktails** *specifically named Plymouth Gin as one of the ingredients. The ABV was reduced in the 1980s to what was considered a more palatable 37.5 percent, but nobody bought it, so they raised it to an 'Original Strength' of 41.2 percent. Thankfully, one may still purchase the 57 percent Navy Strength version, a bottle of which Gustav is said to hold aloft every sunset on a Sussex hillock in deference to the gods of gin. Eyewitness accounts say that Olly tends to sit quietly on his nearby favourite bench sipping from a hipflask.*

FOR THE PERFECT GIN & TONIC:
Fill an ice-cube tray full of Fever-Tree tonic water and freeze in the normal way. Deploy in your next G&T and, unlike standard ice cubes, rather than dilute the drink this method reinforces the flavour right to the final sip. Olly's late Grandpa was a man on a mission to convince the world that the traditional ratio of less gin to more tonic was incorrectly inverted. Olly survived his Grandpa's 'gin-uflections' and for chaps, the perfect proportions are ¼ gin to ¾ tonic over the tonic ice described above. As for the garnish, pair it to the gist of the botanicals. For zesty London Dry Gin, lemon is perfect. For Gin Mare try olives, for Williams Chase gin distilled from apples, a slice of apple is absolutely superb.

———————

MORE GIN RICKEY *F. Scott Fitzgerald adored the Gin Rickey, which he made famous in* **The Great Gatsby***. In Chapter 7, at Daisy's request, Tom makes four Gin Rickeys that 'clicked full of ice'. The story continues, 'Gatsby took up his drink. "They certainly look cool", he said, with visible tension. We drank in long, greedy swallows'. Fitzgerald himself is quoted as saying, 'First you take a drink, then the drink takes a drink, then the drink takes you.' At just 44 years old, he was finally taken, with alcoholism notoriously suggested as a contributing factor.*

———————

THE GIN MARTINI

As far as the Gin Martini goes, there are some who believe that holding the bottle of vermouth up to the light and allowing the glass to be illuminated is enough. After rigorous testing and analysis, Gustav and Olly found that they sounded almost exactly like the Three Tenors when wailing old Sinatra numbers in the back of a cab. They also discovered that the quality of vermouth is paramount. Briny Noilly Prat and scented Regal Rogue are among the finer examples, with their distinctive oomph that prevents the Gin Martini from straying dangerously away from its razor sharp edge. We believe that the perfect Gin Martini should by-pass take-off and take you direct to cruising altitude at the start of an evening.

FOR THE PERFECT GIN MARTINI:
The method is simple. Firstly – and long before the appointed hour of sippery – place your martini glass into the freezer. Or better yet, remind the butler to do it. Next, add 1 part top-notch vermouth to 5 parts excellent gin to a cocktail shaker with ice. Shake vigorously until your hands hurt from the cold and serve with a twist of lemon. Before drinking, silently and discreetly mouth the words 'I am the Lord of Gin' (amazingly it makes it taste even better) and show the drink no mercy as you devour it with the intent of an ogre swallowing a sheep.

NEGRONI: The Negroni is perhaps the finest and most sophisticated of all cocktails. It is also among the simplest to make. Equal parts Campari, Belsazar red vermouth and your favourite gin served in a tumbler over ice, stirred and garnished with a twist of fresh orange peel. It is as sweetly bitter as the exhaustion of victory in a boxing ring.

DRESSING FOR DRINK

—◆—

Gin should always, where possible, be consumed in a blazer. The look you're aiming for is Nicholas Parsons on a bender. Don't let the blazer contain any badges or insignia, and don't, for goodness' sake, wear a boating blazer, except when at specific boat club functions. A plain black or dark blue blazer, preferably with brass buttons, double breasted and buttoned up; the shirt is crisp white, the tie in club colours or striped if not a member of a club; grey flannels, black Oxfords. A moustache is not mandatory, but would certainly add tone. You may place your non-drinking hand in one of the blazer pockets, but not in one of the trouser pockets. Finally, one is *never* permitted to wear shorts and sip a Gin Martini; this is as frowned upon as biting a postman.

CHAPTER 9

VODKA

The Stillness of the Wind

'Two drinks and two drinks only may be drunk out of the bottle –
Calvados and vodka. The only difference is that you wipe the neck of
the bottle with the right palm before passing it on, and the Normandy
orchard is the place for Calvados, while vodka never tastes so good
(the left palm, mind) as when swigged in a Russian train that has run
out of fuel between Saratov and Novo-Sibirsk.'

EXTRACT FROM *THE WINE AND THE WAISTCOAT*, PAUL HOLT, 1956

LITTLE HAS CHANGED since Holt stated his views on vodka over half a century ago. Vodka is eminently portable. Around the same time as Paul Holt, Sir Kingsley declared, perhaps fancifully, the existence of Russian vodkas with an alcohol (not proof) content of 96 percent. The justification, said the expert, was that in northern Russian subzero temperatures, anything with a lower alcohol content would freeze in the bottle.

They either have very cold fridges in Novo-Sibirsk, or the 96-percenters were designed to be drunk outdoors, which only fuels vodka's reputation as the drink of manly men in enormous fur hats, standing around a sledge/brazier/bloodied corpse, passing around a bottle of vodka while discussing the thing in front of them.

This is the sort of stuff that vodka brings with it to our civilised drawing rooms and pretentious Swedish furniture-filled bars, and thank goodness. We wouldn't want vodka to be reduced to yet another trendy

spirit for the masses to chuck into glasses of fizzy caffeine-based mixers. With the exception of a few notable cocktails, including Ian Fleming's own personal recipe for a Dry Martini and of course that bounder's breakfast staple, the Bloody Mary, vodka is a drink best enjoyed neat.

In order to produce vodka, you don't have to be a country whose citizens regularly freeze to death while strolling to the local bar, but it certainly helps. There is not much vodka coming out of Spain or Italy. The traditional vodka-producing belt arcs around the north of Europe, conveniently marking all the countries we heave a sigh of relief at not having to visit; instead, we can simply enjoy the superlative vodkas of Russia, Ukraine, Poland, Finland, Sweden and the Netherlands, and feel we have already been there – as long as we drink it properly.

The viscosity of vodka is such that if the bottle is placed in the freezer, the contents will not freeze. You may have to reserve a

special section of your domestic freezer in which to store all your vodkas. It is worth chucking out all those packets of frozen peas, choc-ices and that loaf of bread you keep for 'emergencies', to create a dedicated vodka compartment.

In this compartment chaps should have at least three of the following vodkas whose provenance and spirit base may surprise you:

CHASE VODKA, HEREFORDSHIRE, ENGLAND Elegant vodka from this single estate's own potatoes. Unbeatable served directly from the freezer.

ADNAMS LONGSHORE FINEST CUT VODKA, SUFFOLK, ENGLAND A wheat vodka voted 'the World's Best Vodka' at The International Wine & Spirit Competition 2014. Impeccable over ice.

REYKA, ICELAND Small batch grain vodka with admirable purity (filtered, apparently, through lava rock), a fab drink on its own or experiment with their very own Flame of Love cocktail: 2 parts Reyka Vodka to ¼ part Fino sherry in a martini glass with a piece of flamed orange peel.

Y-TOWN VODKA, OHIO, USA Made from pure cane sugar, stunning in fruity cocktails – try the Y-Town Sunset: 2 parts Y-Town Vodka, 1 part grapefruit juice shaken over ice, poured into a cold martini glass with a splash of grenadine.

666 PURE, TASMANIA, AUSTRALIA Made from Tasmanian barley and charcoal-filtered, this is the first Aussie vodka to win gold at the San Francisco World Spirits Competition.

FAIR QUINOA VODKA, COGNAC, FRANCE (FAIRTRADE) Organic quinoa from the Altiplano Plateau in Bolivia and sugarcane from Belize crafted into a seamless, gluten-free blend in France. International and excellent.

POTOCKI, POLAND With its roots dating back to 1816, this Polish rye-based vodka is splendidly soft and nutty. Our choice for a Vodka Martini.

And, for a widely available staple with a herby twist, **Bison Grass Zubrowka** from Poland is perfectly acceptable.

Despite what the Kremlin might have admitted, vodka almost certainly originated in Poland as far back as the 8th century. The name 'vodka' is a diminutive of *voda*, the word in both Russian and Polish for water, so vodka translates roughly as 'little water'. We can't help thinking that 'ghostly detonation' might have been a more appropriate name, as vodka is such a pale yet potent spirit. Vodka is a pure spirit and can be made from virtually anything, including potatoes, milk, beetroot and even fruit. Some vodkas are flavoured, a trend which began with simple stuff like ginger, lemon, cloves – Stalin's favourite was apparently flavoured with cayenne pepper – but has recently tended towards more bizarre ingredients: chocolate, truffles, chillies, spaghetti hoops, tennis balls (alright, two of those were made up, but it won't be long).

In Russia, Ivan the Terrible, observing vodka's effects on already violent men, opened a string of taverns, or *kabaks*, which served vodka in vast quantities to his *oprichniki* – the special police force that carried out his orders. By 1648, the rest of the population had acquired the taste for vodka and a third of the country's male population was in debt to the state-owned *kabaks*. The natural response from the peasants, when asked to settle their bar bills retrospectively, was to start distilling their own moonshine vodka. Not that difficult, when you consider the aforementioned ingredients.

Peter the Great supposedly knocked back half a gallon of vodka per day but felt that the peasantry should be more abstemious, and created liquor licenses to put a stop to badly made moonshine. Catherine the Great continued his work by making it illegal for anyone other than the aristocracy to sell vodka. One consequence of this was to improve vodka's quality: it was now filtered with charcoal and occasionally flavoured. Tsar Nicholas II finished off the job Peter the Great had started by banning alcohol entirely in 1914. Thus began the lesser-known period of Prohibition; one that didn't involve jazz musicians swigging cocktails out of teacups and quoting F. Scott Fitzgerald, but Muscovite men drinking themselves to death with appallingly distilled bootleg vodka. The authors have not noticed many nightclubs in contemporary Britain celebrating the Russian era of Prohibition. The 1917 revolution was consequently a dry one, but once the teetotal Bolsheviks began to run out of cash, they looked at ways to bring in funds, and by 1925 vodka was not only back on the shelves of state-run supermarkets, but sometimes it was the *only* item on the shelves. During the Second World War, Russian troops were issued with a daily vodka ration, the working man getting such a taste for it again that, by 1958, players in the Russian national soccer team were apparently so drunk they had difficulty scoring goals from more than five yards away.

Vodka, for its stillness in the glass, is in fact a hurricane. Whether you prefer the character of the base to taste through as in eastern-style vodkas, or the more mellow attributes of western-style vodkas, remember the old adage from Olly's Great Uncle Ormolu, especially if vodka is hiding in cocktails: 'Never drink more than you know.'

There are three recommended mixed drinks that vodka finds its happy home in, but not very many more than that.

BLOODY MARY

2 parts vodka, 4 parts tomato juice, 1 tablespoon lemon juice, 1 tablespoon orange juice, 1 tablespoon Worcestershire sauce, 1 level teaspoon celery salt, pinch cayenne pepper.

Stir in a jug with ice and serve to hungover houseguests in preparation for their next hangover. Add a slug of Fino sherry to back up the savoury character if you wish.

BULLSHOT

2 parts vodka, 3 parts beef consommé (easily purchased in a tin), squeeze of lemon juice, dash of Worcestershire Sauce. Serve with ice.

BLOODSHOT

Essentially a combination of the two above recipes: use half consommé and half tomato juice, the other ingredients in the same proportions as a Bullshot. Both these make superlative early-morning shooting drinks and put a bit of a spring in one's step when handling weaponry.

PETER THE GREAT DRINKER

Peter the Great, Sovereign, Tsar and Grand Prince of Russia from 1682 until 1721, and Emperor of Russia until 1725, was as ambitious in his drinking as in his politics. His parties were legendary and guests were not allowed to leave until Peter himself had stopped drinking – which by then was far too late for most. For Peter had a prodigious thirst and was blessed with virtually no hangovers, partly due to his enormous size – he was 6 foot 8 inches tall. In his palace at Peterhof he had built a special drinking den, called Mon Plaisir, to which anyone had to be winched up, as there were no stairs.

But that was just for guests. Peter the Great's real drinking took place among his drinking group, The All Joking, All Drunken Synod of Fools and Jesters – a drunken parody of the Church's ruling committee. Its first commandment was that 'members are to get drunk every day, and might never go to bed sober.' The election of a new 'Pope' for the Drunken Synod involved the 'cardinals' drinking for eight days solid, the minimum requirement being a teaspoon of vodka every 15 minutes, always served by nude servants. Once a Pope had been chosen – a man in his 80s was usually picked for the job – Peter selected an equally elderly wife for him. The happy couple was borne to the church by the four fattest men in Russia, on a cart drawn by bears goaded with metal spikes to anger them. The couple, once wed, was pushed naked into a room to consummate their marriage. And people question the point in having an aristocracy?

DRESSING FOR DRINK

◆

Vodka is only ever consumed in winter, even though it is served practically frozen. Therefore your outfit should consist of an Astrakhan or fur coat with Hussar facings, a black homburg, grey kid gloves, black barathea trousers with button braces, black leather boots with grey spats, and a Meerschaum pipe. Vodka is never drunk seated, and aphorisms or slightly risqué jokes may be uttered after each draught, though a click of the heels, however slight, is considered inappropriate.

ABSINTHE ALIGHT!

There was a time, not so long ago, when absinthe, the Green Faerie, maintained its mysterious grip on our imaginations. A few, but not many, of us knew of a man who had once tried it in Barcelona and was now dead or completely mad. Others had heard absinthe whispered about by wizened old ladies in small, dusty villages in Slovakia but, as soon as any further queries were made, they disappeared into doorways that were not there the following day. Absinthe remained a drink of myth and legend, never to be drunk but only ever to be admired from afar in the paintings of Degas and Picasso.

Then, in the 1990s, absinthe landed in our lives with all the thumping assurance of an Egyptian god returning to Earth demanding that all buildings should henceforth be triangular. In an act of extraordinary collective consciousness, this mythical aniseed-flavoured beverage seemed to arrive in our off-licences and bars from all corners of Europe like a verdant virus. Very quickly a Green Faerie one-upmanship developed: 'Oh, you're still drinking the Czech stuff, are you? I found this amazing brew from Romania/Albania/Ruritania which is fifty times as potent and three times as cheap.' Absinthe became a cause célèbre, guzzled by the gallons in trendy cocktail bars that served it in special glasses with drops of brown sugar enticingly dripped into it through special spoons and even flames. Everything about absinthe was special – but especially the hangovers. It seemed to make you much drunker than other drinks and leave you feeling, the next morning, like one of Picasso's more difficult paintings.

Those of us who were already seasoned consumers of Pernod, Ricard and Pastis 51 wondered what all the fuss was about – surely absinthe was just another clear anis drink that turned cloudy when mixed with water? Et quoi? The reason for this fuss, as we now know, was wormwood. Absinthe is essentially Pernod plus wormwood, the bitterest flavour known to man, a cure of intestinal worms and a symbol of evil since Biblical times. Originally produced by the same company that today produces Pernod and Ricard, absinthe would have continued its smooth journey into the contemporary palate just as wine, cognac and all its other Gallic chums did, were it not for the fact that the French government decided to ban absinthe in 1914 (with the USA, Holland and Switzerland). The reason? French soldiers in the First World War were drinking too much of it and going slightly bonkers. Naturally a sane military is much to be desired, and it was decided that absinthe, rather than excessive drinking, was to blame for their madness. It remained illegal in France until 2000, though not in many other countries and certainly not in tolerant and boozy Blighty.

Absinthe is, it must be admitted, a rather strong drink, averaging 45–74% ABV, and the nature of it encourages reckless consumption. Gustav recalls the distant days of his 20s, when he discovered an entire case of Spanish Absenta on his father's farm in Mallorca, as well as some bottles of vintage cava. There is no name for the drink that he and his chums concocted from the two, and there should never be a name for it. Gustav still twitches slightly around the eyes when the words absinthe and champagne are mentioned in the same sentence (he did it just then, actually).

So it is generally now accepted that there is nothing particularly 'hallucinogenic' or 'weird' about absinthe – it is simply very strong and quite delicious when mixed properly and the sort of drink to which one finds oneself saying, 'Oh go on then, just one more.' Wormwood, however, *is* weird, even though the amounts contained in a bottle of absinthe are negligible. In the Bible, we learn that 'A great star fell from heaven, burning like a torch, and it fell on a third of the rivers and on the springs of waters. The name of the star is called Wormwood; and a third of the waters became wormwood, and many men died from the waters, because they were made bitter.' Spookily, Chernobyl is the Russian word for wormwood. In 2009, the black metal band Marduk released an album titled *Wormwood*. And, furthermore, Shakespeare cites wormwood's evilness when Hamlet responds to a scene within the play he hopes will provoke Claudius's guilt at killing his father by shouting, 'Wormwood, wormwood!' All of this helped to cultivate absinthe's mystique and led to countless bohemians of the early 20th century swilling it for breakfast, lunch, afternoon tea and dinner (and sometimes even at suppertime). Vincent Van Gogh liked absinthe rather a lot, depicting it in paint several times; ditto Degas, Toulouse-Lautrec and Picasso, all of whom stuck with the generic title of 'The Absinthe Drinker', turning it into as recognisable a subject for a painting as a bowl of fruit or a nude lady. Hot on their heels came Hemingway, F. Scott Fitzgerald and Ezra Pound, who enjoyed both the illegality of absinthe as well as its literary and artistic connotations. Absinthe made the heart grow fonder, and set the bohos apart from the bourgeoisie, with their boring wine and dull cognac. It also identified the artists with the common men, who had been absinthe's biggest customers until it was banned.

Today, attitudes towards absinthe have calmed down and it has entered the mainstream. It is a useful ingredient in many retro cocktails, adding a flavoursome zing that nothing else quite manages. You can drink absinthe like pastis, with added water, though without adding a sugar cube you will find it very bitter. The water should be dripped slowly through the sugar cube and some specialist shops sell the spoons for this, with their distinctive triangular flat base, but you can just as easily use a tea strainer. Or you can start the same way, but soak the sugar cube in some of the absinthe and then set it on fire, allowing it slowly to caramelise and drip into the glass. When almost finished, pour ice-cold water on the still-burning sugar cube and it should all blend in the glass into a cloudy, sweet substance. This process is, appropriately enough, called 'louching' and should preferably be done in a very long silk dressing gown with tassels. Or try making Ernest Hemingway's favourite absinthe cocktail, a Death in the Afternoon: 'Pour one jigger of absinthe into a champagne glass, add iced champagne until it attains the proper opalescent milkiness. Drink three to five of these slowly.' (Gustav's eyes did that thing again.)

Does absinthe have a place in a gentleman's drinks cabinet? Yes, as long as the brand is correct, for some of them have become associated with high jinks on stag nights in Prague, and that is no place for a chap. Choose from the following six blends:

PERNOD ABSINTHE RECETTE TRADITIONNELLE (68% vol)
Launched in 2013 and based on records from the 1800s, Pernod updated their own original recipe only by improving the quality of the ingredients: the wormwood sourced from the fields of Pontarlier, and, instead of colouring it with nasty dyes as in the old days, they used macerated botanicals such as stinging nettles. The result is a more refined version of what used to turn French soldiers mad, and the only mad thing about it is the price.

VIEUX PONTARLIER (65% vol)
Like the new version of Pernod Absinthe, the ingredients come from the original wormwood fields of eastern France near the border with Switzerland.

LA CLANDESTINE SUISSE (53% vol)
Another Suisse-styled absinthe, made in the birthplace of the spirit, Couvet, in the Val-de-Travers region of Switzerland.

ROQUETTE 1797 (75% vol)
Based on a late 18th-century recipe, when absinthe was closer to a medicinal potion, this takes the drink to more complex levels of flavour.

DOUBS MYSTIQUE (65% vol)
The Doubs region of eastern France is the historical home of French absinthe, and Doubs Mystique Carte d'Or is distilled in the century-old alembic stills in Pontarlier.

Absinthe has the impact and power of a Gatling gun firing aniseed balls into your solar plexus. Both absinthe and the revolving Gatling barrel can be lethal when pointed into one's face, but only one of these, to our knowledge, has ever been reconditioned to play gramophone records in *Carry On Up the Khyber* – which is exactly the kind of gently jolly and surreal vision a really splendid absinthe ought to inspire.

suspect that a chap's courage could only ever be enhanced by rum - up until the point of snoozing in a hammock below decks to sleep it off, of course.

TOTTY *A tot – also known as a totty – should best come from the command to 'splice the mainbrace', which can only be initiated by The Queen, a member of the Royalty but sometimes the Admiralty and by other notable powers in the Common-wealth. Usually reserved for marriages and births of the Royal kind, but we at Chap HQ would like to see it expanded to include every birthday of Ellen MacArthur, Royal Siren of the Waves.*

Rum has throughout history retained a curious sense of a commodity to be traded, stolen and even deployed to grease the political rails. George Washington is said to have given out around 28 gallons of rum and 50 gallons of rum punch to some 391 voters, while running for his seat in the Virginia House of Burgess. It cost him fifty quid, but he won. With fond memories, he insisted at his 1789 inauguration on cracking open a barrel of Barbados rum. History does not report if he swilled the lot before roaring, 'Now THAT'S power.'

Cuba may not be the most important rum producer today – most of what comes out of illegal stills slips into the shadows as the local moonshine – but all the best rum drinks still bear that nation's name: the Daiquiri is named after the place where liberating American forces, who fought off the occupying Spanish, first landed in 1898. They brought with them a new drink called 'Coca-Cola', and thus was born another legendary cocktail, the Cuba Libre (which is absolutely NOT just rum and coke, but a far subtler blend of rum, Coca-Cola and fresh lime juice). The name means 'Free Cuba'.

So rum went from being gargled by pirates and presidents and grogged by sailors into the tall glasses of sophisticates in the 1950s, but it was still a very basic drink - Captain Morgan and Bacardi often being the only brands available in the UK until fairly recently. Today one may purchase a bewildering variety of rums, most of which are more than good enough to be sipped neat or washed down with a splash of water. Small tulip-shaped glasses are the best vessel for sipping rum neat, and our preferred glass would be filled with Ron Zacapa Solera 23, fractionally blended in a solera system in Guatemala in a method usually deployed by the creators of fine sherry.

It is definitely worth having a bottle of clear rum in one's cabinet, for the making of essential Daiquiris, Mojitos and Cuba Libres. Incidentally, Hemingway was a fan of Mojitos and boosted their fame by sipping them at La Bodeguita del Medio in Havana as well as in Florida. Legend has it that he preferred champagne to the usual addition of soda. The cad.

In Paris and Berlin one may easily find rum bars, where no other spirit is sold, such is the proliferation and sophistication of this tipple today. Gustav and Olly, rather than moan about the absence of such splendid establishments on Blighty's shores, silently and solemnly unpack their rum supplies at Henley Regatta every year, allowing themselves one Royal Naval rum ration for every vessel in every race they are about to watch. Neither of them is the nominated driver home.

Rum, for every chap, ought to be considered less of a by-product of the sugar industry and more as the reason why sugar cane exists. And since the only thing you really need to make it according to regulation is a bit of sugar cane growing locally, rum production is rising in the Philippines, Australia, South Africa and beyond. Rum is on the rampage.

HOT BUTTERED RUM

Trader Vic, the most famous cocktail-maker the world has ever known and who gave his name to countless 'tiki' bars in the 1950s, bequeathed a lot more than roomfuls of bamboo furniture and coconut shells for glasses. His recipe for Hot Buttered Rum remains the definitive one:

40ml dark rum
boiling water
For the 'batter':
455g brown sugar
115g butter
½ teaspoon ground nutmeg, cinnamon and cloves
Pinch of salt

Beat the above ingredients into a paste, then add a heaped teaspoon of it to the dark rum and some boiling water, with a cinnamon stick for decoration.

Sir Kingsley was a huge fan of this warming winter concoction and drank it in defiance of the advice of David A. Embury, author of *The Fine Art of Mixing Drinks*, who declared: 'I believe that the drinking of Hot Buttered Rum should be permitted only in the North-west Passage, and, even there, only by highly imaginative and overenthusiastic novelists.'

NELSON SWIMMING IN RUM
Admiral Lord Horatio Nelson was tragically removed from his own victory celebrations after Trafalgar by being dead. Most of the time, sailors who snuffed it were heaved over the side straight into Davy Jones' Locker with a few words of calm reflection or curses, depending on whether they snored like a gargling whale and kept the entire crew awake voyage after voyage. Nelson's body, however, was preserved in a vat of rum, and the story goes that, when the ship made port in Blighty, the vat had been sipped dry by his shipmates wanting a taste of his 'spirit'. Nelson's Blood is a spiced rum drink with over 100 ingredients, which you can still find today in the pub in Burnham Thorpe, Norfolk, the village where Nelson grew up. Previously known as 'The Plough' the pub was renamed in his honour 'The Lord Nelson' in 1798. Olly has visited many times and revels in the unique character of this ancient drinking house, which mysteriously has no bar, only a tap room from where the drinks are served.

DRESSING FOR DRINK

◆

Rum should be consumed in a rather crumpled linen suit that seems to contain multiple shades of off-white. The shoes should either be white canvas deck shoes or a pair of espadrilles bought locally (you should ideally be in Cuba, Dominican Republic or any other troubled Caribbean island nation). The hat should be a Panama that looks as if Fitzcarraldo himself had dropped it into the Amazon several times and fished it out again. The only accessories required are a gold signet ring and a very large cigar with a slightly chewed end.

CHAPTER 12

COGNAC, ARMAGNAC
& the Dreams of the Devil

AT A DINNER of cardinals, a very long time ago in Rome, Monseigneur Cousseau was apparently asked which See he represented. 'I am Bishop Angoulême, Bishop of Charente,' he proudly stated, to completely unimpressed silence from the other bishops. He quickly added, 'And Bishop of Cognac.' The audience soon responded gleefully: 'Ah. Cognac. What a glorious and superb diocese!'

Such is the power and mystique of this superior French tipple. The sun, so they say, never sets on a bottle of cognac; it is seen as the drink of kings, emperors, suddenly rich rock stars and other men who frequently wear fur. Cognac is to wine what whisky is to beer – the more intense, arresting, deep and much more expensive older brother. Cognac is traditionally consumed from enormous balloon glasses, by men with enormous embonpoints and vast cigars, in cavernous rooms draped with damask and history. But, in fact, all cognac should be sipped from small tulip-shaped glasses to maximise the aroma and minimise the fiery effect of the alcohol.

Cognac featured heavily among the favoured drinks of Churchill during his ceaseless campaign to destroy Nazism during the Second World War – and ironically was almost certainly one of the drinks most enjoyed by the more dissolute members of the Waffen SS. (The Führer himself preferred orange squash, apparently.) An inspection of the cellar at Chartwell in the 1950s revealed extensive supplies of Hine brandy, among other cognacs and lots of other booze. During the privations of the First World War, Churchill had written: 'We live very simply, but with all the essentials of life well understood and pro-vided for – hot baths, cold champagne, new peas and old brandy.'

Brandy is the spirit distilled from wine and can come from anywhere in the world. But just as there are mass-produced pairs of jeans that no self-respecting chap would ever lace around his legs, so the finery of the specific regions of Cognac and Armagnac are the prime appellations which chaps should readily dunk their tongues into. And none other. For simplicity, fun and sheer wonderment, we shall compare these varied and underrated spirits with fictional TV detectives from Bergerac to Morse. The truth is, all of these spirits taste slightly different depending on the base wine, the character of the still, the way the spirit is divided, nurtured and collected and finally how it is matured, in what and for how long. Exactly the same as TV detectives: some improve with age and become the defining ilk of their genre (Joan Hickson's Miss Marple) while others are cast by the wayside as the years recede (Dempsey and Makepeace). And the biggest fact that should be etched behind every chap's eyeballs is that too much of this stuff can have exactly the opposite effect of Asterix's magic potion and render you a cantankerous wicked devil wreathed in dreams of dark brooding, yet scholarly destruction. Take heed.

COGNAC

Cognac is the appellation north of Bordeaux and is famed for its enduring, mesmeric and elegant yet eccentric variety. It is widely regarded as the finest of all brandy but, as we shall see, overlook armagnac at your peril. Cognac has six districts – here they are in descending order of quality, which we have likened to television detectives. These are your first ports of call on a cognac label.

GRANDE CHAMPAGNE: The Jeremy Brett of Sherlock Holmes. Very fine.
PETITE CHAMPAGNE: Joan Hickson's Miss Marple. Refined pedigree.
BORDERIES: Prime Suspect. Decent.
FINS BOIS: Inspector Morse. Thoroughly good.
BONS BOIS: John Nettles as Bergerac. Surprisingly watchable.
BOIS ORDINAIRES: Cadfael. Nuff said.

These districts more or less radiate out from the town of Cognac itself, with the soil of the finer ones exhibiting a high chalk content, considered better for the grape, and of the lesser ones becoming more sandy, especially towards the Atlantic. A great all-rounder for a chap to memorise is a further category on the label, '**Fine Champagne**', which is a blend of both Grande and Petite Champagne with at least 50 percent Grande. It can be compared to the work of David Suchet as Hercule Poirot, which straddles mainstream and refined. All this talk of champagne, it should be noted, has absolutely nothing to do with the sparkling wine region. In fact the grapes planted in Cognac are completely different, in the main consisting of Ugni Blanc, which is rather neutral and high in acidity, making it a perfect candidate for distillation.

In 1909 a decree protecting the delimited area of Cognac was drawn up, stating that only the spirit made with eaux-de-vie from this region and using permitted grapes may be given the name cognac. Furthermore, cognac must be double distilled in a copper alembic and aged in oak barrels for a minimum period of time.

So, to put it succinctly, all cognac is brandy, but not all brandy is cognac.

AGES

Cognac is aged in oak barrels, with the top stuff sometimes referred to as ageing in 'paradis', or paradise, a special place in the distillery for the really splendid booze to quietly age and evolve. Say it how it is, chaps! Some cognacs are shipped to Britain to be aged because the cooler climate allows a slower maturation and these are labelled 'Early Landed'. The age of a Cognac is guaranteed for the first six years of its life as follows:

*** or VS, Very Special – two years old

VSOP, Very Special Old Pale, Very Superior Old Pale – three years old

XO, Extra Old – generally six years old

Hors d'Age (meaning 'beyond age') officially is the same as an XO but almost always implies further ageing and a high grade.

In practice, reputable merchants can provide cognac from single years and they stretch back into the depths of centuries gone by. For his 40th birthday in 2014, Olly bought a bottle of 1914 Cognac Hermitage Borderies with which to toast and mark the event. It proved to be a very moving bottle to open, 100 years after the start of the First World War.

But cognac doesn't have to pre-date two world wars in order to be fabulous. One way of testing a good cognac is to wet the inside of a glass with it, then empty it, preferably into your mouth. If the cognac is good, the aroma will remain in the glass for hours, even days.

One of Olly's oldest tastings was of an 1805 cognac – the year of Trafalgar. The astonishing thing about such bottles is that they are intact and drinkable in the first place. But the remarkable truth was just how fresh it tasted – lip-smackorous with a kick of booming pineapple and a deep rumble of nutty richness. Consider those grapes, growing in 1805 with the sunlight and rain of that year under open skies of southwest France. Who picked them? What was it like at the harvest? Which of them were in love? Where did the grapes go? Who distilled them? How did the barrel survive and imagine the feuds, affairs, births, wars, rivalries and risks that wreathed the barrel across the centuries before it found its way into a bottle bound for England, into Olly's glass and finally into his face at which point he became tangibly at one with a substance more than two centuries old. It's altogether transporting.

CHURCHILL *Churchill himself estimated that by 1945, aged 71, he had drunk enough brandy to fill three railway carriages.*

NAPOLEON *The Little Corporal loved the stuff and the term Napoleon ought to refer to a Cognac that's the same age as an XO, a minimum of six years. Even so, we'd always pick an Hors d'Age – shorthand for 'off the official age scale' and denoting very high quality – from a reputable seller.*

Movement is important to cognac; it was the region's proximity to Bordeaux (the vineyards of Cognac pretty much continue north from the Bordeaux vineyards) and the River Gironde that led Cognac up towards England. It was found that the light white wines made from Ugni Blanc didn't travel well, but fire them up into a spirit first mentioned in 1549 and boom, the entire character of a region was born. The 1800s brought Cognac's biggest phase of development, with key families such as the Martells from Jersey, the Hines from Dorset and the Hennessys from Scotland moving in and taking command. While these names are widely available, it is worth seeking out the smaller producers, whose bottles vary hugely in character but offer a lexicon of pleasure to chaps who are prepared to taste their way to nirvana.

ARMAGNAC

————//————

As with Cognac, the region of Armagnac has unique properties. While larger producers may be tempted to doctor their distillations by adding, for example, caramel to enhance colour, we urge all chaps to take the path less trodden and seek out smaller producers. Armagnac is located much further south than Cognac and lies inland, so that it does not benefit from the moderating effects of a maritime position. The vineyards are warmer, which gives rise to a slightly richer, more prune-like flavour from the grape varieties grown in Armagnac – mainly Ugni Blanc, Colombard and Baco. Thanks to this climate, the wines from Armagnac are of better quality and can be sold as Côtes de Gasgogne. Armagnac probably has a longer history than cognac, perhaps as far back as the 12th century when the Moors brought their knowledge of distillation to the region. Today, the districts in descending order of quality are as follows:

BAS ARMAGNAC. The best. Often sold single vintage and with the name of the domaine. This is Armagnac's answer to Magnum P.I. – fulsome and manly. If it could grow a moustache, it would.

TÉNARÈZE. More of a robust flavour. Like Luther, it could beat you in a fist fight.

HAUT-ARMAGNAC. Gives the best wines from chalky soil, which ironically makes them the least suitable for distillation. A Touch of Frost. Popular, but by no means fine.

ARMAGNAC AGES

*** – at least two years old

VSOP Very Special Old Pale – five years old

XO Extra Old – over six years old

You can also find vintage Armagnac from a single year, Olly's got a bottle of 1974 from his birth year that seems to magically top itself up every time he takes a sip.

OTHER BRANDIES FROM AROUND THE WORLD

SPANISH BRANDY

The region for Spanish brandy is Jerez in Andalucía, where sherry is also made, and its official title is Brandy de Jerez. It is aged in sherry casks using the 'solera' system, which involves adding the brandy to successive barrels as it ages, each one containing an older spirit, so that the new one takes on the essence of the old one while retaining its youthful vigour. A bit like teenagers hanging around with their parents while on holiday, then moving on to the local nightclub when they get bored. Once a Brandy de Jerez has aged for three years, it's called a Solera Reserva. After ten years its title graduates to Solera Gran Reserva. The most commonly used grape variety is the Airén, though a dash of Pedro Ximenez is often added too, giving a much deeper sweetness. Spanish brandy's main difference from French cognac is its sweetness, hinted at by its much darker, richer colours. Some names to look out for are:

Cardenal Mendoza
Gran Duque d'Alba
Lepanto
Carlos I Solera Gran Reserva

GRAPPA

Distilled from the pomace, the solids that remain after the grapes have been pressed, this Italian spirit comes in all sorts of guises depending on grape variety and whether it has been oaked. A quality grappa – even after ageing in oak – can be a surprisingly pleasant digestif and can even taste rather splendid as opposed to just pleasingly warming.

MANHATTAN *Henry Hudson's third attempt to find the fabled Northeast Passage in 1609 reached land and encountered the Delaware Indian tribe. Hudson shared his brandy with the Chief who, it's reported, passed out. The tribe also got stuck in and called the land 'Manahachtanienk', which more or less translates as 'the place where we got totally pie-eyed'. As every chap will concur, Manhattan has certainly lived up to its name.*

'Claret is the liquor for boys; port, for men; but he who aspires to be a hero must drink brandy. In the first place, brandy is most grateful to the palate; and then brandy will do soonest for a man what drinking *can* do for him. There are, indeed, few who are able to drink brandy. That is a power rather to be wished for than attained.'

SAMUEL JOHNSON

DRESSING FOR DRINK

◆

Cognac. Either full Grenadier Guards mess kit or a Siren Suit. If neither of these is available, you'll have to stick to Armagnac, for which you may wear Mufti.

LEGENDS OF LIBATION
Peter O'Toole

'I can't stand light. I hate weather. My idea of heaven is moving from one smoke-filled room to another.' Thus spake one of Hollywood's most successful imbibing thespians. Peter O'Toole lived to 81, only surviving two decades of hellraising with his dipsomaniac cohorts Richard Harris, Richard Burton and Ollie Reed by giving up the booze in 1975. Before that he stored up enough drink-sodden anecdotes to keep him going on the chat show circuit for a lifetime.

On one epic session with Peter Finch in Ireland, the pair wanted to continue drinking at a small local pub, but time had been called. Their solution was to buy the pub, O'Toole bringing out his chequebook and asking the landlord to name his price. The following morning, after sobering up, the pair rushed back to the scene of the crime. Luckily the landlord hadn't cashed the cheque and disaster was averted. O'Toole and Finch remained friends with the pub owner, and when he died his wife invited them to his funeral. Both knelt at the graveside as the coffin was lowered in, sobbing noisily. Only when they both looked up did they realise they were at the wrong funeral; their landlord friend was being buried 100 yards away.

O'Toole was a man who carried his chequebook wherever he went, but never a watch, a wallet or his house keys. 'I just hope some bastard's in,' he'd say. More than once he had to explain to the police why he was breaking into his own property.

He was born in 1932 in a rough neighbourhood in a small town in Connemara, Ireland. Three of his playmates were later hanged for murder. 'I'm not from the working class,' O'Toole used to say. 'I'm from the criminal class.'

Thesped at RADA, O'Toole was cast in 1959 in *The Long And The Short And The Tall* at the Royal Court Theatre. His understudy was a young Michael Caine, and one Saturday night after the show the pair went to a nearby restaurant. Eating a plate of egg and chips was the last thing Caine remembered, until he woke up in broad daylight in a strange flat. 'What time is it?' he asked his drinking companion. 'Never mind what time it is,' said O'Toole. 'What f***ing day is it?' It was five o'clock in the afternoon, two days later. Curtain call was at eight that evening. When they hurried to the theatre, the manager informed them that the restaurant owner had banned them from his establishment for life. Caine wanted to know what they could possibly have done, but O'Toole said, 'Never ask what you did. It's better not to know.'

Ten years later, O'Toole was filming *The Lion In Winter* with Katharine Hepburn. During a scene on a lake, O'Toole trapped his hand between two boats and lost the top of a finger. He carried the tip back to shore, dipped it in a glass of brandy to sterilise it and then bandaged it back on to his hand. Three weeks later, he unwrapped it to find that he'd applied it the wrong way round, having finished off the brandy while he'd fixed the finger.

'I did quite enjoy the days when one went for a beer at one's local in Paris and woke up in Corsica,' said the actor once, also admitting it wasn't until 'around 1985' that he became aware of President Kennedy's assassination.

O'Toole was just as passionate about the gee-gees as the booze. During filming of *The Great Catherine*, director Gordon Fleming sent an assistant to fetch the actor for a scene. The assistant found the dressing room empty, but a television set was showing horseracing from Sandown Park, not far from the studio. The TV camera zoomed in on the crowd, and there was Peter O'Toole cheering on the horses.

In 1975, when O'Toole was 43, an abdominal irregularity he'd persistently ignored ('My plumbing is no one's business but my own,') finally erupted and he was rushed to hospital for a major operation. 'It was a photo-finish, the surgeons said,' O'Toole declared after a long operation. There was so little of his digestive system left that any amount of alcohol could prove fatal. He never touched another drop and made it to 81, outliving all his peers from his drinking days, but never losing his wit: 'When did I realise I was God? Well, I was praying and I suddenly realised I was talking to myself.'

CHAPTER 13

WHISKY, WHISKEY & SCOTCH

L ET'S START by clearing up one of drink's great mysteries with a single blow: it's spelled 'whisky' in Scotland and most of the world, but 'whiskey' in America and Ireland, with the exception of a few producers such as Maker's Mark in the USA, who are presumably jolly proud of their Scottish ancestry. The Japanese word for it is *Uisukī*, but it's pronounced 'whisky'. There, that wasn't so hard, was it?

Humphrey Bogart's last words, so the story goes, were 'I should never have switched from scotch to martinis'. We are slightly perplexed as to why a choice had to be made in the first place. Surely the weather, mood, company and circumstance should dictate the drink in your glass? Anyhow, we raise ours to Bogie and his enduring love for Scotch. But what exactly is Scotch?

SCOTCH, GRAIN AND MALT

Scotch whisky is a spirit blend fused from a number of Scottish distilleries. The two types are grain and malt. Grain is mainly maize from a patent still; malt is malted barley usually from a pot still. You can of course find 'single' whiskies – malt and grain – which are the work of one single distillery. Scotch. Malt. Single. Done.

Between the 11th and 13th centuries, the 'water of life', which became known as 'whisky', from the Gaelic *uisge beatha*, came to the shores of Ireland and Scotland with Christian monks. With the dissolution of the monasteries, many monks set up on their own in Scotland and, in a flurry of warming sips and knowing grins, distilleries began to sprout like hair from the palms of a barbarian. Very soon the words 'Scotland', 'Whisky' and 'Hurrah' all became synonymous.

MALT

Similar to the beer-making process, malt whisky begins with tricking the barley (malt) into germination, a technique known as conversion – almost exactly like Bruce Wayne turning into Batman, the starch is converted to sugar. Because Bruce is usually wearing a starched shirt and Batman is … sweet? Hang on, this metaphor doesn't work at all. It's more like Prince Adam turning into He-Man. No, the Princess turning into a pea. Base metal into gold. That's it, base metal into GOLD! In any case, before it goes and transforms too far and wastes energy on sprouting, the malt is toasted in a kiln. Sometimes peat is burned for heat, as in Islay malts, which gives the whiskies their characteristic intensely smoky flavour. The ground malt is mixed with warm water to create a mash, which is brewed (again,

similar to beer) and then double and sometimes triple distilled. The core of the distillate (the 'heart') is used with the 'heads' and 'tails' heading back for further distillation. The most important thing, however, is that you drink many bottles to discover which sort you like the best. Whisky, like gymkhana in the nude, is an intensely personal pursuit.

All kinds of other things impact the final flavour of the whisky, from the barley itself to the water, yeast and character of the still itself. But the biggest impact comes from maturation – in what and for how long. For three years while it languishes in oak casks, the substance is officially called British Plain Spirits, until finally it can be called whisky. But the character of the cask whether it has previously been filled with sherry, bourbon or indeed if it's simply a second-fill whisky cask, will also give nuances to the final dram.

WHAT'S IN A NAME?

Well, in the case of whisky, a name can give the reader an idea of regional distinction, which can also be broadly clumped into groups of flavours.

HIGHLAND AND ISLAND are whiskies from north of Greenock and Dundee that range in flavour from peaty to floral. Old Pulteney belongs in every chap's reach.

SPEYSIDE whiskies are fine, elegant and classy from near the River Spey. Look out for Tamdhu, which Olly was honoured to re-open some years ago after a period of dormancy known as 'mothballing'. It tastes splendid and feels as mellow as Gustav crooning his Ballads of Love to the Moon.

ISLAY bottlings tend to be bold and smoky. Get your chops around Lagavulin and know what it feels like to actually be a bonfire. Phwoar!

LOWLAND malts are the lightest and often used for blending. Glenkinchie is worth a squirt for starters. In fact several squirts. How many squirts to a deluge? We've lost count.

> 'The water was not fit to drink. To make it palatable, we had to add whisky. By diligent effort, I learnt to like it.'
>
> WINSTON CHURCHILL

HOW TO TAKE IT

Take it like a chap – however you feel best. There's much made of the purity of whisky and how it should only ever be doctored by a splash or two of water, or else you'll be eternally damned by the gods of booze. The truth is, Olly has spent many an hour carousing with master distillers and, as Gustav has also discovered on his extensive safaris around Whisky Island, everyone has a different opinion. Over ice, with soda, or, in the case of the master distiller at Dalwhinnie who recommended this to Olly in person: straight out of the freezer with a square of dark chocolate. Not at all sacrilegious, in fact sublime. And what do the master distillers themselves enjoy drinking? A fair number in our ken are secretly partial to the old classic Johnnie Walker Black Label. It's always good to have a widely available option up every chap's sleeve and there is no shame in sipping what the fellas who make it secretly toot.

Sir Kingsley, however, has fixed views on this: 'If your host is mad enough to offer you ice or, better still, drop it in unasked, you get bonus points for the way you manage to restrain your horror at the fellow's barbarism.'

BOURBON

————//————

Bourbon is arch-cad and lothario Don Draper's tipple of choice and it differs from other American whiskey (note the addition of the 'e' and then let's stop talking about that) as it must be made from at least 51 percent corn and matured in charred new oak containers, which accounts for its mellow sweet tinge. 'Straight' Bourbon is the stuff for chaps – aged for at least two years. Old Granddad is fantastic value, top quality and a brilliant example of spicy bourbon with a high rye content. Woodford Reserve is mellower and widely available, and works rather well as part of an Old Fashioned (sugar lump, angostura, bourbon, ice, fruit – generally orange). Craft distilling is on the up, with excellent examples such as FEW, who make belting bourbon in Illinois. On the more traditional side, look out for Old Forrester and Fitzgerald's 1849. As with Scotch, a square of dark chocolate makes an admirable partner and, as for cocktails, the Mint Julep, the Manhattan and the Old Fashioned should all fall within a chap's simple lexicon of cocktails to be made when blindfolded and tied to a barstool with leather belts.

AN ODE TO WHISKEY 'For whiskey belongs to the world, to the sky, to the earth, to you. Whiskey is not something in a bottle. Whiskey is no devil's brew, hatched in a cauldron called a laboratory. Whiskey is of Mother Earth – whiskey is a grain, product of sun and wind and rain and cool nights and even little burrowing animals; whiskey is water, the magic thing of the seas around us and the heavens above, the thing we carry in our bodies and call blood, the sound of running brooks over smooth rocks, the crash of waterfalls, the sight of rainbow and dew and mist and thunderhead.' *ESQUIRE DRINK BOOK, 1957*

Don Draper, Mad Men

Most bourbon is made in Kentucky, but in fact you can make America's native spirit anywhere in the country. And, as every chap knows, Jack Daniels is not bourbon but Tennessee whiskey that's been filtered through charcoal known as 'The Lincoln Country Process'. And if you've ever wondered what 'sour mash' means on the JD label, it's nothing to do with flavour, just a system of keeping a consistency from one fermentation to another. Talking of consistency, when Olly visited the Jack Daniels distillery, he was astonished to discover that the distillery is located in a *dry*

county, in the town of Lynchburg, to be precise, which is the seat of Moore County, the smallest county in Tennessee. Despite housing one of American's most famous distilleries, it's been dry as a bone since Prohibition. You'll be pleased to hear that Olly, in the Great British tradition, managed to keep perfectly wet at all times, thanks to a combination of his innately piratical nature and a discreet veneer of English charm. Frank Sinatra was a big fan of Jack Daniels, which he enjoyed sharing with Roger Moore. You could always tell when it was party-time at Frank's house – the Jack Daniels flag

would be hoisted above Twin Palms and, as a matter of fact, Frank was even buried with a bottle of Jack snuggled next to him ... just in case. As Frank put it so admirably, 'Alcohol may be man's worst enemy, but the Bible says love your enemy.' We couldn't agree more.

If an American whiskey has 'Rye' on the label, it must be more than 51 percent rye, but in Canada there is no restriction to the proportions of grains used.

> 'Always carry a flagon of whisky in case of snakebite, and furthermore, always carry a small snake.'
>
> W.C. FIELDS

———————

Alexander Fleming, the brain box behind penicillin, was supposedly said to take 'a good gulp of hot whisky at bedtime – it's not very scientific, but it helps.' Olly and Gustav, when tucked up in bed and reading to one another in their annual 'sip 'n' share' festival, tend to add hot water to a splash of whisky with a slice of lemon studded with a few cloves, and sugar to taste. It usually keeps them up all night. That and the fear that one of them might have smuggled a weapon beneath the eiderdown. One year Gustav whipped out a medieval ball and chain and it caused huge mirth when Olly revealed he too had smuggled in exactly the same instrument of death! How they laughed, though the dog didn't.

———————

THE LONG WAY HOME *Vaudeville actor W. C. Fields allegedly hit Long Island with a pal to pick up some bootleg booze during Prohibition. On the return journey, Long Island seemed to get longer and longer, until they finally sobered up in Florida. Gustav did exactly the same thing in 1996 but travelling in the opposite direction.*

IF BY WHISKEY *In 1952, Judge Noah S. 'Soggy' Sweat Jr. gave a world-famous speech on the nature of whiskey to the Mississippi State Legislature, which at the time still enforced Prohibition. The whiskey speech apparently took 2½ months to write and was received with tear-stained eyes by those on both sides of the argument. In the end, it was 14 more years before Mississippi finally allowed its liquor stores to fling open their doors again. On 6th August 1966, local newspaper the* **Delta Democrat Times** *ran a front-page headline that simply read 'Happy Day'.*

Highlights of the speech were the following lines:

'If when you say whiskey you mean the devil's brew, the poison scourge, the bloody monster, that defiles innocence, dethrones reason, destroys the home, creates misery and poverty, yea, literally takes the bread from the mouths of little children; if you mean the evil drink that topples the Christian man and woman from the pinnacle of righteous, gracious living into the bottomless pit of degradation, and despair, and shame and helplessness, and hopelessness, then certainly I am against it.

'But, if when you say whiskey you mean the oil of conversation, the philosophic wine, the ale that is consumed when good fellows get together, that puts a song in their hearts and laughter on their lips, and the warm glow of contentment in their eyes; if you mean Christmas cheer; if you mean the stimulating drink that puts the spring in the old gentleman's step on a frosty, crispy morning; if you mean the drink which enables a man to magnify his joy, and his happiness, and to forget, if only for a little while, life's great tragedies, and heartaches, and sorrows; if you mean that drink, the sale of which pours into our treasuries untold millions of dollars, which are used to provide tender care for our little crippled children, our blind, our deaf, our dumb, our pitiful aged and infirm; to build highways and hospitals and schools, then certainly I am for it.'

CANADIAN WHISKY

Prohibition in the USA was invigorating to Canadian distilleries north of the border. Rye survived Canada's harsh winters more successfully than other grains which is how it came to be so significant in the blend, generally giving light whisky that's got punchy flavours wreathed in spice. Although Canadian whisky is sometimes referred to as 'Rye Whiskey', it's not necessary for rye to feature but commonly it'll lead the blend boosted by barley and corn, which must be aged for more than three years. The Detroit River was so busy during Prohibition that it became known as the 'river of booze'. Now that's where every chap should be taking the waters! Today there are distilleries from east to west, such as Shelter Point in the west, Glenora in the east. Canadian Club is probably the most famous along with Crown Royal but we recommend ordering Canadian single malts whenever you spot them. They're not common but they can be gloriously characterful. Glen Breton Rare 10 Year Old is a great example that we're stalking through the bars and booze shops of this world like a big game hunter about to pounce. Or be pounced on. Where whisky hunting is concerned, you never can quite tell … .

IRISH WHISKEY

Many are happy to hand out the prize for being the first nation to distil whiskey to the Irish, though naturally the Scots contest this. The Bushmills distillery in County Antrim was founded in 1608 and is the world's oldest licensed distillery. Glenturret and Bowmore in Scotland can make credible claims to have been founded in 1775 and 1779 respectively, though Ardberg, Oban and Blair Athol are equally historical, if more difficult to place a precise date on. The fact is that none of us really cares who started making whisky or whiskey, nor indeed how they spell it, we are all simply grateful that some frightfully clever coves once, a very long time ago, decided to start chucking malted barley into a pot still and watch it turn into the water of life.

What matters today is that, should you prefer a slightly smoother whiskey, then reach for the Bushmills, Jameson or Midleton and pour yourself a large one. However, should you require something more complex, be aware that Irish whiskey is growing and changing faster than you can say 'Make mine a double and keep that ice bucket well away from the glass.' Styles of Irish whiskey are now far more wide-ranging than ever – look out for the new wave of distillers such as The Dingle Distillery on the west coast and Teeling over in Dublin. There are single malts coming out of Ireland, including Tyrconnell and Connemara, as well as peatier, Scottish-style infusions. And, hear this curious though totally factual fact: Irish whiskey is the fastest-growing spirits category in the world! And, before you ask, Irish coffee is entirely acceptable to chaps. In fact, is there any other type of coffee? No. There isn't.

JAPANESE WHISKY

In 1918 Masataka Taketsuru came from Japan to Scotland to begin an apprenticeship in Chemistry at Glasgow University. His ambition was to learn the secrets of Scottish whisky distillation and export them back to Japan, where he would set up his country's very first commercial whisky distillery. Principally studying the habits of those running the Hazelburn distillery in Campbeltown, Taketsuru spent five months observing every detail.

But Taketsuru did not just return to his homeland with an intimate knowledge of whisky, but also with a wife. During his travels around Scotland, his heart had been stolen by a bonnie lass named Jessie 'Rita' Cowan and, against her parent's wishes, Taketsuru had married her and taken her back to Japan. It took him longer to find an investor than a wife, but eventually a wealthy entrepreneur named Shinjiro Torii understood the potential of distilling Scottish-style whisky in Japan, and in 1924, construction began on Yamakazi, Japan's first-ever commercial whisky distillery, on the outskirts of Kyoto. This particular site was chosen due to an excellent natural water supply, from three sources: the Katsura, Kizu and Uji Rivers. In 1929, the year of the Great Crash in America, Yamakazi's first whisky was released, White Label, with the catchy slogan 'Wake Up! The time has gone when you have to appreciate imported goods. Now, for the first time, superb domestic whiskies are available in Japan.' It must have worked, for White Label is still in production today, nearly 100 years later, while Hazelburn distillery is not.

More distilleries followed, and by the 1970s there were 13 Japanese distilleries. There are now eight, but they are all internationally recognised and are frequent winners of global whisky awards. Japanese whisky is normally distilled twice, as in Scotland, using pot stills. The barley used is mainly imported from Scotland, though some from Australia. American oak bourbon casks are also imported from Scotland and America, along with sherry casks from Spain. Sometimes Japanese oak barrels are used, giving more Japanese characteristics to the whisky.

The climate in Japan is closer to that of Kentucky and Tennessee in America than Scotland. This means much greater extremes of temperature during maturation for the whisky, resulting in faster rates of maturation. One of the effects of this is a slightly woodier final flavour. In a typical example of the Japanese refining imported techniques, they have designed differently shaped stills and, by varying the type of yeasts used for fermentation and experimenting with cask maturation, each distillery is able to achieve a much broader range of flavours than a Scottish distillery.

SELECT JAPANESE WHISKY DISTILLERIES

CHICHIBU: operational since 2008 to the northwest of Tokyo, it is the newest distillery in Japan. All their equipment was imported from Scotland.

EIGASHIMA: founded in 1888 near Kobe to produce sake and shochu, it branched out into whisky production in 1984.

FUJI-GOTEMBA: based at the foot of Mont Fuji, it is the world's largest whisky distillery at the time we wrote these words, rather than when you are reading them. See? Time travel is possible.

HAKUSHU: the highest distillery in Japan,

it is situated around 2,300 feet (700 metres) above sea level and produces three million litres of whisky a year.

KARUIZAWA: the smallest distillery in Japan, it is based in a mountain resort, where the water used has flowed through volcanic lava rock, giving their award-winning whisky a unique flavour.

MIYAGIKYO: principally known for their blended whiskies, their small batches of single malt have consistently won World Whisky Awards.

YAMAZAKI: still going strong after its auspicious beginnings in 1929.

YOICHI: is situated on the island of Hokkaido, which has the same land area, the same population and similar climate conditions to Scotland. Spooky but true, and good for the whisky, one of which won the most prestigious prize of 'Best Single Malt' at the World Whisky Awards in 2008. Yoichi was the first Japanese whisky to win this coveted award and this was seen as the beginning of Japan's entry into the world whisky market.

The success of Japanese whisky on the international stage has encouraged projects the world over, including in England, such as the London Distillery Company – London's first whisky distillery for over a century. Every chap should consider it his duty to try, if not all of the global whiskies, then certainly most of them. After all, whisky, like chaps, comes in all shapes and sizes and with such a pleasurable challenge to benchmark the lot, where's the downside?

DRESSING FOR DRINK

◆

 The ideal outfit for consuming whisky is a kilt, but for the Sassenachs among us, it is one of the more flexible drinks, sartorially speaking. A dinner jacket is one option, and you will have reached the stage of the night when the bow tie may be loosened (see Cocktails, dress). An entirely different approach would be a three-piece tweed suit in a heathery shade of green or lovat; pocket watch, eight-sectioned tweed cap, in a different shade to the suit, white shirt, tartan tie (but not a tartan relevant to you in any way), Tricker's brown brogues or Grenson brogue boots.

CHAPTER 14

LIQUEURS & CURIOSITIES

From Pisco to Disco

Picture the scene: elegantly attired guests at your home sit around a partially destroyed dinner table, subtly pushing their chairs away to make room for their newly acquired embonpoints. The table is littered with the debris of a fine repast, some of it arranged by one of the guests to re-enact the battle of Trafalgar using bread baskets (Napoleon's fleet) and gravy boats (Nelson's fleet); various cheeses lie in ruins and no one can be bothered to awaken the guest who dozed off during the last-but-one *trou normand*.

Port has been passed, cognac consumed and plumes of smoke rise from enormous Cohibas. Your English guests have lit their pipes. The atmosphere is one of serenity, sated calm and replenished souls. Yet, as the host, you still feel inadequate, and wish you could serve your guests a final *coup de grâce,* for which they will remember the repast even more fondly than those incredible angels on horseback.

This is when your supply of liqueurs will come into play. Your cabinet of curiosities should contain at least several 'cups of grace', which can be served in small yet impressive quantities, which will leave a lingering taste on buds that have been pushed to the limit of human endurance. However, be fully aware that, if served in too great a quantity, these power potions and tremor tonics will transform your cup of grace into the chalice of regret come dawn. Be warned. Read on. And drink.

There is a vast quantity of liqueurs available and it is not recommended that you acquire them all. Otherwise you will simply accumulate lots of sticky bottles with one glassful missing, the recipient of that lone serving not even having finished his over-sweet concoction in a peculiar colour.

The essential six liqueurs worth being in possession of are the following:

COINTREAU/COMBIER/ GRAND MARNIER/ TRIPLE SEC

These are all pretty much the same fiddle bashing out a similar tune with a different bow, triple sec being the generic name while the other three are brands. Combier and Cointreau have made claims to being the first triple sec and both are worth having in the drinks cabinet, as is Grand Marnier, which is layered with a few jazzy extras. Apart from a few old ladies who don't really like drinking at all and may actually request a Cointreau, the principal purpose of this orange-flavoured liqueur is in the making of cocktails. A Manhattan, for example, without triple sec is like a car without an engine or a house without a billard room.

CHARTREUSE

—————//—————

According to legend, only two Carthusian monks know which 130 or so herbs and plants are used to make green Chartreuse, using as their guide a 400-year-old manuscript. Each year some 18 tons of these herbs are delivered to the Grande-Chartreuse Monastery in the French Alps north of Grenoble. After being dried and crushed, they are taken to the distillery in nearby Voiron and turned into Chartreuse, a bright green liqueur with no added colouring whatsoever. (There's a yellow version too, which is milder and sweeter, but it's the green you want.) The main reason for chaps to drink it is that, in *Brideshead Revisited*, the narrator Charles Ryder drinks Chartreuse after dinner with Anthony Blanche, who declares that it's 'Real G-g-green Chartreuse, made before the expulsion of the monks. There are five distinct tastes as it trickles over the tongue. It is like swallowing a sp-spectrum.'

Chartreuse is a curious liqueur, in that it continues to evolve once bottled. Some say keeping it for decades improves it. Olly and Gustav couldn't say – whenever their 'green mist' descends, it usually lasts for several days of passionate chatter by which time the contents of the bottle are neatly dispersed into their resonant faces.

KAHULA

—————//—————

A coffee-flavoured liqueur might seem like a strange choice for a gentleman's drinks cabinet, but we are not talking about an Irish Coffee cream liqueur – and we will never be talking about that. Where those are beige-coloured concoctions, Kahlua is a dark coffee liqueur entirely meaningless on its own. If any of your guests specifically request it when they see it on the bar, flatly refuse to serve it straight. The only reason to keep Kahlua in the house is for making White or Black Russians. There are very few occasions when either colour of these wonderful cocktails is not appropriate; the only drawback is that the black variety requires the addition of Coca-Cola, which you'll have to ask a child to locate for you in some dreadful shop. The White Russian is, of course, the preferred goblet-filler of Jeffrey 'The Dude' Lebowski. While more of a fella than a chap, Gustav and Olly cannot help but doff their double-fedora to his passion for Kahlua. The double fedora, incidentally, is the only such example in the world and proves beyond doubt that a) standing 'shoulder to shoulder' does not always mean fighting and b) two heads are invariably better than one.

DANZIGER GOLDWASSER

Created by Dutch Mennonite inventor Ambrose Vermollen in 1598 in Danzig, today Gdansk in Poland. Back then it was part of Germany, which is not really important; what is important is that Herr Vermollen put 23-carat gold flakes into his heady concoction of 19 different herbs and fruits, creating an alcoholic legend. At the time, gold was believed to have medicinal properties, whereas today we know it has only financial properties, which makes this bizarre drink all the more decadent and pointless. It is also the prime ingredient of a Pousse Café, which we do not advise you to try and make on a full stomach. Better on a full bank account.

SLIVOVITZ

Slivovitz is a clear brandy made from plums, versions of which are found all over Eastern Europe: in Serbia it is the national drink; in Albania it is a form of currency; and in Poland it is known as a penance for one's sins. Slivovitz is one of the few alcoholic drinks considered Kosher during Passover, when grain-based drinks are forbidden. It is very strong: 100–140 proof (50–70 percent ABV), and is traditionally drunk in shots, while standing in the snow over a corpse, uttering some short, sharp Slavic requiem. It works equally well among living chums at the dinner table.

PISCO

Pisco is a South American grape spirit made by distilling fermented grape juice. Both Peru and Chile claim to have invented it and both countries export various brands of it. The Spanish brought Quebranta grapes to South America to make wine with, and Pisco was made with the leftover grapes. Today there are three main types of Pisco, but only *pisco puro* is made from a single grape variety, originally Quebranta. Alcholado is a blend of different grapes. Mosto Verde is made from partially fermented grape juice. There are oak-aged Piscos but for us it's like wearing two dressing gowns where one, or none, will suffice. In all its forms, Pisco packs a punch and is more palatable in cocktails, notably the Pisco Sour – pisco, lime juice, whizzed up egg white and a dash of Angostura Bitters – created in the 1920s by American bartender Victor 'Gringo' Morris at The Morris Bar, Lima. After a late night sampling various bottles of Pisco, Olly is now the only man alive in possession of the domain name 'piscodisco.com' but he has absolutely no idea what to do with it.

OTHER ALCOHOLIC ANOMALIES

The above are the required liqueurs for your drinks cabinet, but are there any other beverages we have not mentioned in all our other chapters in this extensive and exhaustive tome? Are there any drinks that simply do not fit into any particular category like beer, wine, whisky or gin, yet still have a certain presence in the glass and certain moments when they are the perfect tipple? Well of course there are, and of course we are going to tell you what they are.

DUBONNET

Dubonnet was created by Parisian chemist and wine merchant (the two jobs used to be interchangeable) Joseph Dubonnet in 1846, as a way of making quinine more palatable for the French Foreign Legion battling malaria in North Africa, much in the way gin and tonic was used by British troops in India. Dubonnet and gin was the Queen Mother's favourite tipple, and the same cocktail is also enjoyed by our current Lady Monarch. We can think of no better reason than this to keep a bottle in your drinks cabinet, just in case of a surprise Royal visit. Once, the staff at Lord's Cricket Ground nearly came a cropper when they couldn't find a bottle of Dubonnet before a Royal visit, and we believe one should always keep a slightly better cellar than Lord's. Olly had lunch in the presence of the Queen in 2015, having been presented to Her Majesty earlier in the day. During the lunch, Olly is 99 percent certain that The Queen enjoyed a discreet Dubonnet. But he would, of course, never reveal it.

CAMPARI

Campari is a marvellously energetic homage to the bitter flavour of the scented orange. You can serve it neat over ice, top it up with orange juice, soda water, or kink it into various concoctions, but the salient point to make is that it is altogether marvellous. For fans of Campari, Aperol too is a must – the Aperol spritz of Aperol, soda water, prosecco, ice and a slice is a supreme summer beverage that, while delicious taken on a warm Italian sojourn, is equally splendid in the kitchen after a troubling day at work.

GINGER WINE

Olly's partially teetotal granny swore by ginger wine and indeed it is a drink that enhances the very soul such is its sweetly warming splendour. Blend it with whisky for the Whisky Mac, which was favoured by Olly's grandfather who was massively not teetotal.

TEQUILA

Agave is the oddly fleshy plant that creates the naughty spirit forged in the volcanic hills of Tequila, Mexico, which has been a UNESCO heritage site since 2006. You'll be aware of the large industrial producers whose names most chaps should ignore and whose work has caused many of us to experience thunder in the mind the next morning, but the best tequila comes from 100 percent blue agave and, amazing but true, the flavours vary according to how the spirit is aged. Blanco is unoaked and the finest bottles give a gently scented herby flavour similar to rosemary, and are easy and warming rather than burning with alcohol heat. **Reposado** bottles are aged for between 2 and 11 months in barrel, **Añejo** for 12–35 months, while **Extra Añejo** is aged for over 36 months. In general, old whisky or bourbon barrels are used and, as tequilas are aged, they assume more savoury flavours and a darker colour. Whichever style explodes your piñata, always check the label states '100 percent agave' to be sure you're getting the quality that befits a chap. Gustav and Olly reckon that the top-end small batch tequila producers crafting their fine spirit in masonry ovens with natural agave yeast are fit to rival some of the best producers of cognac, whisky and rum the world over. And we should know, we've spent many hours bathing in the stuff. Agave does wonders for the skin. Though we do not recommend you try this at home. To be clear, we are joking. To bathe in tequila is madness when it can be liberally sipped. Although now we've raised bathing in it we can't get the idea out of our heads. Blast.

DRESSING FOR DRINK

In order to mark the shift away from the consumption of food, and enter the midnight arena of post-prandial peculiarities, you should change out of your dinner jacket and into an opera cape. This will signal to your guests that you are about to serve them drinks that will probably blow their minds. By all means wear a top hat too, and perhaps flourish a walking cane with a handle made from an intricately carved elephant's testicle or some such.

CHAPTER 15

HANGOVERS

A HANGOVER is to a chap what a tin of dog food is to a gourmand – generally to be shunned, unless there is no alternative. Where booze is concerned, excess is to be by-passed in favour of the ring-road to sheer quality. But on that rare occasion when the devil has lured you to sip from his armpit and judgement has been superseded by your insatiably lustful primal thirst, you will be banished from yourself – albeit for a few long horrible hours. Deal with it. Gibberish has been spouted from fonts of hope throughout the ages regarding a cure for the hangover, but Gustav and Olly can tell you without hesitation that time and a slow drip feed of cold clear mental regret are the greatest healer for those who have sipped from the Chalice of Thunder. That and drinking plenty of water.

Our neat, dual-pronged suggestion for tackling the situation once and for all will be revealed. First of all, forget the fried breakfast, it will only make you full – your greatest challenge is to re-focus your mind. Where once a lake of clarity beamed precision, wit and curiosity into the skies of your mind, now a kaleidoscope of self-pity is wreathed in the stench of your wretched frailty. You are experiencing self-banishment. Your challenge is to refocus your mind and seize control of it before your mental dignity dissolves permanently into indelible droplets of self-doubt. Be speedy and commit once again to ruling your mind as you would a plate of beef. First of all, through language, for by naming and owning the situation, your chances of conquering the far shores of Survival Island are greatly improved.

THE LANGUAGE OF HANGOVERS

The language of hangovers reveals a curious spectrum of colourful descriptors for that unique feeling of toxic time travel:

In Norway they say, 'Carpenters in the head'. The French call it 'Wooden face'. In Germany it is 'The wailing of cats'. In Chile the phrase translates as 'I have the monkey'. Spain has the poetic 'Pulling back of the wave' but Kingsley Amis nailed it in *Lucky Jim* when he wrote: 'A dusty thudding in his head made the scene before him beat like a pulse. His mouth had been used as a latrine by some small creature of the night and then as its mausoleum. During the night, too, he'd somehow been on a cross-country run and then been expertly beaten up by secret police. He felt bad.' You feel bad? Act fast.

IDIOTIC HISTORICAL CURES

NB *Some of these don't work. One of them might.*

The ancient **Greeks** apparently swore by boiled cabbage – the strong smell allegedly helping to restore the senses. Might as well smoke a 15-year-old cat turd.

The **Romans** wittered on about raw owl's eggs or a deep-fried canary. Frankly this is why their empire deserved to fall.

Drinkers of the Middles Ages favoured a bitter almond or even a raw eel. At least it wasn't leeches.

Charles II is supposed to have taken Goddard drops, created by a bloke who said they had 'a few irrelevancies added, such as skull of a person hanged, dried viper, and the like.' Sounds almost exactly like Gustav making ratatouille.

Nicholas Culpeper in the 1600s came up with the idea of squirting ivy juice up the nostrils. A sensualist *and* a pervert.

Chimney sweeps of the 1800s are said to have added some soot to warm milk. Cretins.

In 1824 **The Medical Adviser** suggested pouring vinegar down the throat and rubbing it into the temples, or if that didn't work out 'let him be stripped, and have a pail of water showered on him from three feet above his head.' Olly does this every day before his constitutional stride. It is not strictly a hangover cure, merely a way to greet the day and lay down the challenge to the gods to make it a belter.

The Victorians are reputed to have mixed up 11 drops Peppermint water, 5 grams Sulphate of Iron, 10 grams Magnesia, 1 drop Spirit of Nutmeg. Surely more of an aperitif than a cure for over-indulgence?

In *Jeeves Takes Charge*, the ever-creative butler comes up with Worcestershire sauce, raw egg, and pepper for **Bertie Wooster**. 'Gentlemen have told me they find it extremely invigorating after a late evening.' Personally, we find donning a jet-pack and firing up the boosters for a skyline sojourn across the Sussex Downs even more invigorating. Especially after – or perhaps even during – a late evening. But we might just about give Jeeves' suggestion a go.

CURES FOR CHAPS

———//———

Olly's most unusual experience of a liquor-storm cured was during a visit to the vineyards of Santorini, when a combination of orange juice, black coffee and omelette, a volcano and Tina Turner's *We Don't Need Another Hero* pumped at the volume of an ape falling from an aeroplane restored normality in spritely style. However, our two most valuable suggestions are simply these and in this order:

A shave
The gardening

Why these two seemingly menial tasks? Because, friends, when one is hungover, one has disconnected from the Tree of Life. Casting one's mind back to the Night Before, one may dimly recall being at one with the Universe, at one with one's chums and at one with whatever was in the glass before one.

But, during the hours of fitful and perspiring slumber that, the Morning After, now divides you from the Night Before, something horrid and unthinkable has happened. You have been separated, in some ghastly divorce of the mind from its moorings. This is what Kingsley Amis called the Metaphysical Hangover. You went to bed, or rather tumbled into the nearest horizontal repository, perhaps a sofa, a pile of coats or a ditch, with a smile upon your face and the lines of your favourite poetry or song ringing in your ears, having ended the evening by regaling your companions with the fruits of your fecund and extremely awakened mind.

Now, the decree absolute has been handed out. While your former drunken self keeps the house, the money and the children, your sober self is left to reside in a filthy bedsit, where you will lie in agonised wait for a reunion. Thankfully not for long. By the early evening, all will be well again and the happy family of you, your mind and even your slightly damaged body will be reunited, in the pub. Then it starts all over again.

Garden, my friend. Connect with the earth. Build a bonfire. Get your hands dirty and work up a sweat. If you haven't got a garden, do it in the bath. Heat has incredible effects on hangovers, which is why we hardly seem to notice them while in hot countries or near beaches (or is that because we are on holiday and don't care?). Take an extremely hot bath, as hot as you can take it without removing a layer of skin; a long, leisurely shave with a best badger shaving brush – but not the cut-throat, not today. An hour later, an absolute slathering of the fizzog with all the unguents in your bathroom cabinet (including the cough mixture and the Night Nurse) and you will look and feel, if not like a million dollars, then at least a tenner better than you did when you awoke.

DRESSING FOR DRINK

◆

It may seem anomalous to dress for a hangover; after all, you are supposed to be paying penance for all the well-dressed carousing of the previous night. This, however, is a schoolboy error. Spend hours in the bathroom, having the closest shave of your life, smother yourself in beautiful smelling unguents and colognes, and lay on your bed the finest suit of clothes you possess. Tie a particularly splendid knot in your tie; give an extra shine to your shoes. Stepping forth into the world dressed like this will do wonders to ease your hangover, even if on the inside your entire organism is still reeling with horror.

DRINKING
AND CRICKET

——//——

In *Cricket, a Coaching Manual for Boys*, Somerset's gentleman cricketer M.D. Lyon observed that 'half a glass of beer won't hurt you … and a cigarette, or better still a pipe, is comforting'. Leicestershire's A.G. Steel preferred shandygaff, sherry or claret when on the job. As a rule, gentlemen, as opposed to players, favoured aperitifs or spirits. Colin Ingleby McKenzie had a penchant for Hadfields (a drink similar to Pimm's), which was Lord's very own concoction. When Trevor Bailey played there in a 1955 Test, despite advertising Lucozade, he rounded off the luncheon interval with four cognacs. Batting shortly afterwards he perished for 13, complaining he was unable to concentrate.

During the 1934 Old Trafford Test, Gubby Allen limbered up with a whisky and soda. His stuttering opening over contained three wides and four no-balls. Northern fast bowlers generally stuck to bitter, with Harold Larwood routinely sinking half a gallon during a day's play.

A siege mentality operated for campaigns on the subcontinent. In the 1950s some Indian states banned booze, so the England players exploited a loophole and registered themselves as certified alcoholics. This guaranteed them a personal allowance of a couple of dozen bottles of a beer or three bottles of spirits a month.

Naturally, we turn to the Australians for drinking tales that involve lager. Walrus-moustachioed David Boon holds the Australian drinking record for a Sydney-to-London Ashes flight, consuming a staggering 52 cans of beer. What isn't that well known is how Rod Marsh's assault on the record had ended a few years earlier. The wicket-keeper knocked back 45 cans but, unlike Boon, who strolled off the plane seemingly as sober as the pilot, Marsh was comatose. So comatose that team-mates Dennis Lillee and Graeme Wood loaded him on to a luggage trolley and wheeled him through customs – the 'nothing to declare' side of course.

During the 2013/14 Ashes tour, England were ridiculed for issuing an 82-page list of their dietary requirements, ranging from 'mini mushroom and spinach bhajis' to 'quinoa with roasted butternut squash, apricot and parsley'. It's a far cry from the banqueting of W.G. Grace who, when touring Canada, enjoyed the local delicacy haunch of bear. The prescribed refreshments for Alastair Cook's outfit were fruit juices and smoothies. This wouldn't have washed with Douglas Jardine's Bodyline tourists. During the campaign, future England captain Freddie Brown did the honours as twelfth man. He recalled his tray always included 'Two brandies and soda, one whisky and soda, three glasses of Champagne, two pints of beer for Larwood and Voce, and a glass of milk for Eddie Paynter'.

When the 1954/55 Ashes squad set sail for Australia, they were issued with a medical booklet, *Cricket in Hot Climes* by Dr. Butterfield in which the author advised them, when socialising, to stick to 'weak drinks' such as beer, lager and wines. He added that if you are determined to drink heavily, 'dilute your spirits well with soda water or ginger ale or tonic water'. If jaded the following morning the recommended drill was 'Take two Alka-Seltzers. Try to take some breakfast. Lie down for half an hour after breakfast. Don't smoke yet.'

Kent batsman Gerry Weigall lived his life by a curious set of maxims such as 'Never drink port after Champagne' and 'Never eat pie at a cricket lunch.' Once at an MCC match he had to go hungry after both steak and kidney pie and apple pie were proffered.

Spectators at Lord's enjoy picnicking in the coronation garden, though nowadays limits on alcohol have made it a bit of a poor show. The MCC only permits two pints of beer or one 75cl bottle of wine per individual. For C.B. Fry this would have been practically an aperitif. When reporting on a Test, his provisions included reserve hampers of hock and chicken sandwiches – in case there has been a strike by caterers. He'd also bring a copy of *Herodotus* and a box of Henry Clay cigars. At midday he'd hand out to guests his own concoction, a stiff cocktail christened Bamboo-shoot, which was a tumbler filled with equal measures of gin and whisky.

C.B.'s lunch consisted of lobster washed down with a fine Traminer '26. When encountering a lady who needed bucking up, Fry dispatched a page to the Langham to fetch a bottle of Liebfraumilch (then considered a top-notch wine) of a suitable vintage. The lad was given strict instructions to drive back in a taxi that never exceeded 15 miles an hour.

WITH THANKS TO STEVE PITTARD

THE THREE TYPES OF DRINKER

The three characters that may be observed consuming each of the major drinks. Give yourself one point for each one you spot in your local hostelry.

COCKTAILS
Al Capone
Sir Roger Moore
Tara, bubbly but dim intern from
    PR company

BUBBLY
Charles Heidsieck
Lilly Bollinger
A cavalry officer after Le Sabrage

WHITE WINE
Three identical young women in a bar

RED WINE
Henry VIII from his famous red wine
    fountain
The connoisseur
The hipster from a stemless glass

FORTIFIED WINE
A gouty old colonel with his nose
    dangling in a large glass of port
A stick-thin fashion journalist sipping
    neat red martini
A youthful Spanish partygoer sipping a
    small glass of cold Fino

BEER
- A youthful male hipster with an immaculate beard sipping craft beer
- A pot-bellied CAMRA member with a less immaculate beard
- An Australian

CIDER
- A summery teenager
- A farm hand
- A Norman

GIN
- A gin lane harridan, from the bottle
- A British ex-pat, from the Rotary Club bar
- A naughty MP, from the Back Benches

VODKA
- James Bond
- A model
- Vladimir Putin

ABSINTHE
- Gustav
- A green fairy
- Van Gogh

RUM
- A pirate
- A sailor of the Royal Navy
- Lord Nelson bathing in it (while dead)

COGNAC
- Churchill
- Napoleon
- O'Toole with his severed finger

WHISKY
- A monk
- Father Jack
- Captain Haddock

LIQUEURS
- Jeffrey Lebowski with his White Russian
- The Queen Mother with Dubonnet
- Anthony Blanche with Green Chartreuse

TYPES OF DRUNK AND HOW TO DEAL WITH THEM

THE ANGRY CHILD 'Don't look at me in that funny way.' If this phrase is uttered in a pub, and its bearer is touching you in any way at all, and especially if tugging on your sleeve, it is time to make good your escape. The Angry Child is usually male, though lady versions exist, and can suddenly spring out of nowhere.

One minute you're carefully laying a round of drinks on the table and catching the tail end of your companions' conversation, the next there is an angry pair of eyes boring into your soul, after you make an innocent remark such as, 'Yes, I've always found it rather warm in Sicily.'

'Are you a fascist?' is the sort of remark that the Angry Child will open with. They mainly speak in questions, as if they wish to receive confirmation that everything in the world really is as awful as they perceive it to be. In reality, it is their interior self-loathing that is causing this, but that won't help you when your red-faced interlocutor is tugging at your sleeve.

There are two responses to the Angry Child. One is to make light of his rage by brushing it aside and saying, 'Come come, old chap, let's change the subject from twenty-first century cannibals to which crisp packet designs have changed the most.' However, this rarely works. A much more effective response is to treat the Angry Child like a real angry child, and shove some huge boundaries around him: 'Finish that drink and then leave us.' This works if you have the bottle. Less terrifying is, 'We're going to another pub now and you're not coming because we're scared of you.' Then run away.

THE REPETITIVE REPEATER

'My mother always wanted to visit the Languedoc.' If an uncommon phrase keeps emanating from a corner of your group at the pub, which has gone a bit quiet over the last hour or so, and then is repeated several times, you have a Repetitive Repeater on your hands. These come in equal measures of male and female. They cannot hold their drink and are relatively harmless, but should really go home.

Endlessly replying with words such as 'So you were saying' won't work, as they don't know they are repeating themselves, and you yourself end up as a Repetitive Repeater. It is, after all, a stealthy condition, that like yawning can be unwittingly transferred from one drinker to another in a single sip. The best tactic is to persuade them to change places with someone so that they are sitting right next to an Irrelevant Informant. Then the two drunks simply cancel each other out.

THE IRRELEVANT INFORMANT

'Bees are the only insects unable to walk sideways.' With such mind-blowingly tedious utterances will the Irrelevant Informant announce his arrival in the group. Whatever the conversation, he or she (usually he) will sweep it off the table and plant his non-sequiturs firmly in its place, refusing to allow anything remotely interesting to be said by anyone. Having a drink with them is like having a drink with a packet of cornflakes, and not even in the days when they came with surprise figures hidden inside them.

The only way to deal with the Irrelevant Informant is to beat him at his own game. Then sprinkle in a few nonsensical facts among a litany of incredibly tedious ones, thus catching him off his guard. EG 'Vegetables can speak.' 'Disc jockeys never wear underpants.' 'Yoghurt is illegal in Singapore'. Be brazen, show no shame and, if push comes to shove, detonate this unfailing torpedo at the I.I. by leaning in, lowering your voice and, in your very best conspiratorial whisper, firmly declare that 'cows dream of freedom'. Wink, stand up and climb out of the window.

THE SINGER OF SONGS

These days, the Singer of Songs is a breed rarely encountered and one almost has a fondness for them, for they were slightly better than the blaring music pumped into most pubs today. However, the Singer of Songs does tend to silence a group and all conversation must cease while the others listen to his song, which might go on for hours if not stopped. The songs he sings are nearly always in a dialect of some sort, whether Irish, Scottish, or some obscure region you have never heard of.

The correct facial expression to adopt when the Singer of Songs is in full flow is a sort of twisted half smirk, but don't think your awkwardness will stop him or her. The S.O.S. is the most seasoned, confident performer and, whether the audience are enjoying his 20-minute rendition of 'The Bonnie Hoose O'Aerlie' or not, he will not care a fig and will keep going until time is called. He can only be stopped with a counter attack: learn the words to a Portuguese folk song or, even better, a Korean Death Metal song, and simply launch into it when the Singer of Songs is in full flow. Drunken song-singing etiquette dictates that he must stop and allow you to sing whatever you like. Your godawful song will soon put him off the whole idea of singing in pubs, possibly forever.

THE DARK STRANGER

The Dark Stranger (aka The Shadow) is the lumpy, leaden force of social suffocation that has the social skills of a gorilla and the annoyingly powerful presence of a car made of eyeballs. You cannot evade their first strike and they will attack repeatedly. Typically, they meander throughout a party or pub, always solo and with no motive other than to speak and compete. The Dark Stranger's hidden flaw is a grotesque shard of inadequacy which twists into the heart and erupts in competitive conversational boulders. 'Why are you drinking that crap?' 'It's all about you, isn't it?' 'I bet I can guess your email address' and so on.

T.D.S. is fundamentally tortured into regarding everything as a potential source of envy or self-comparison, which wrecks chat like a matchstick galleon in a hurricane of farts. One option to cut the bout short is simple rudeness. 'You don't have to talk to me' delivered with the dead eyes of a seagull on a sandwich, works rather well, but can inspire further ire and jealousy such as 'Not good enough for you? I'd look better in that cravat if I tied it round my balls'. The only true antidote to The Dark Stranger is to deploy the Fake Phonecall. Take out your mobile, hold it your ear, get up and say 'Hello? Cooper! I thought you were in Jamaica? How wonderful to hear from you…' Get to your feet and find a ring of friends to corral and defend against further attacks. Be warned, The Shadow will return repeatedly and with all the charm of a yo-yo dunked in manure.

THE MAUDLIN MISERY

The Maudlin Misery is the unique strain of drunk that hits a seam of wanton gloom and just keeps on pecking, like a pigeon in a bag of week-old chips. 'It's bad enough doing January, but February just takes the piss' is the kind of gentle opener to expect. The M.M. will amp things up as the drinks go down, occasionally casting for sympathy with lures such as 'I can't even put my own socks on anymore' but you must never ask why, ever. The Maudlin Misery cares as much about you as you should about the tirade of self-pitying nonsense that brews up inside him like yeast in a humid bin.

The M.M.'s mental traffic is strictly one-way and if he had a mantra it would be 'nobody even wants to understand me'. The truth is, we all understand the Maudlin Misery only too well. 'No you don't, you can't even remember my middle name'. The fact is, he adores moping in imaginary cul-de-sacs, where things aren't so much devastating as just not quite as good as had been hoped. And as soon as M.M moves from beer, cider or wine to spirits, expect dewy eyes and a repellent level of attention-seeking wreathed in a vortex of shame.

10 PHRASES FROM THE
DRUNKEN DICTIONARY

———— // ————

One for the road?
I've had enough.

What are you staring at?
I'm desperately lonely, please will you be my friend?

I love you.
I've no idea who you are.

There's no beer left.
It's my round.

I'm not that drunk.
My eyes don't work.

I wish I could be more like you.
You're a cretin.

I'll never drink again.
See you here, same time next week.

Really?
Please stop speaking.

I've missed my train.
Perhaps we should make love?

I'm just having a rest.
Send for my sedan chair.

———— // ————

INDEX

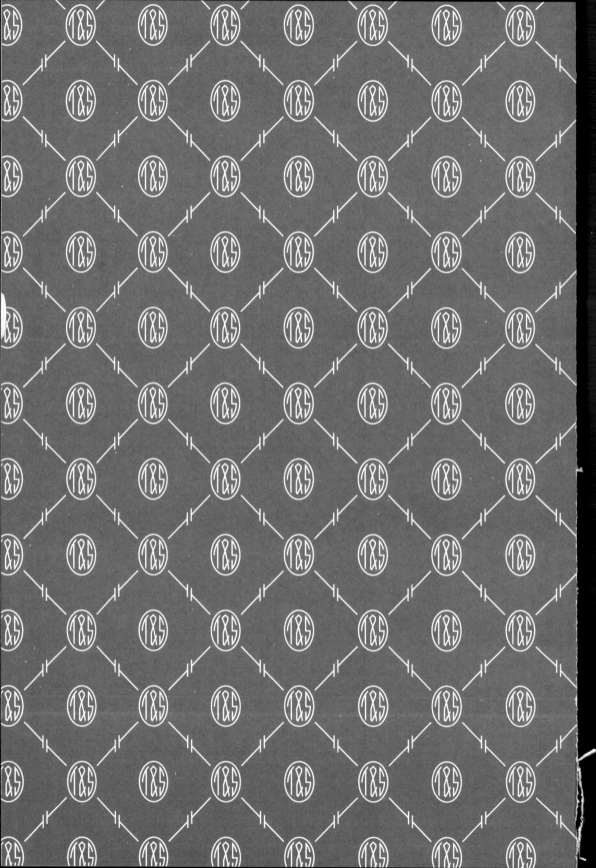